SAMSUNG GAL

USER GUIDE FOR PROS

A Comprehensive Step-by-Step Instructions on How to Use Samsung Galaxy S23 Ultra with Professional Tips and Tricks Like a Pro

GOLDEN MCPHERSON

Disclaimer!

"The information provided within this Book is for general informational purposes only. While we try to keep the information up-to-date and correct, there are no representations or warranties, express or implied, about the completeness, accuracy, reliability, suitability or availability with respect to the information, products, services, or related graphics contained in this Book for any purpose. Any use of the methods describe within this Book are the author's personal thoughts. They are not intended to be a definitive set of instructions for this project. You may discover there are other methods and materials to accomplish the same end result."

TABLE OF CONTENTS

INTRODUCTION 1

Samsung Galaxy S23 Ultra 1

Design 1

Display 2

Specifications 2

Camera 3

SAMSUNG GALAXY S PEN 4

CHAPTER ONE 5

INSERTING THE SIM/ MICRO AND NANO 5

INSERT / REMOVE SIM CARD 5

REMOVING A SIM OR MEMORY CARD 6

How to Remove an SD Card 6

POWERING ON/OFF THE DEVICE 7

The Galaxy S23 ultra can be turned off using the collection of buttons. 7

Making use of the Quick Settings menu. 9

Forcefully restart a stalled Galaxy S23 Ultra 10

USING THE QUICK SETTING PANEL 11

Making use of the Quick Settings 13

Rearrange the button location. 17

Flight mode 20

MAKING USE OF THE SIDE AND VOLUME KEYS 21

The volume Key 21

Side key 22

GPS Antenna 22

CHAPTER TWO 23

SAMSUNG GALAXY S23 ULTRA SETUP 23

How to restart or switch off the Samsung Galaxy S23 ultra 23

THE HOME SCREEN 23

AVAILABILITY OF CONNECTIONS 26

    How to Configure eSIM.. 26

    Utilizing Samsung DeX 26

    Link to Windows 27

    You can personalize Android Auto on Samsung devices 27

    Utilizing Digital Assistants... 28

    WAYS TO DISABLE GOOGLE ASSISTANT 28

Lock screen as well as always display... 31

Security and unlocking... 33

DO NOT DISTURB, VOLUME CONTROLS, AND SOUND 34

    Learn how to adjust the media volume.. 35

    Change the overall vibration intensities... 35

    Utilize Convert music to alter the sound output 36

    Enable "do not disturb" option for notifications............................... 36

    RECOMMENDED BATTERIES 37

CHAPTER THREE... 39

SAMSUNG ACCOUNT CREATION 39

    Configuring an account in Setting.. 39

    Your Samsung account management.. 39

    How to customize your content in Samsung services and applications.............. 40

CHAPTER FOUR 42

HOME SCREEN AND APP DRAWER 42

    View of the Home Screen in nature 42

    Manage Home screens 43

    Control Wallpaper 43

    ADD OR REMOVE FOLDERS 44

    DELETE OR ADD WIDGETS 46

    The widgets can then be changed by swiping left and right. 47

    Replace the apps in the section of your preferred apps. 47

Why would you ever want the applications folder disabled? 49

How can the applications folder be replaced using "Search from Home Screen"?
.... 49

WAYS OF NAVIGATION 52

Change the type of navigation panel... 52

PERSONALIZING HOME SCREENS 54

Tips.. 57

NOTIFICATION PANEL 57

Setup notification preferences. 58

Activate or deactivate notification badges... 59

Activate or deactivate lock screen notifications.. 59

Toggle notifications on or off for each individual app.. 60

Refine the notification sounds... 61

EDGE PANEL AND ITS USAGE... 62

Activating the Edge Panel 62

Making changes to the edge panel handle... 66

CHAPTER FIVE 68

CONTENT TRANSFER WITH SAMSUNG SMART SWITCH........................... 68

Part 1 68

Part 2: 68

IMPORT iCloud Contents 69

Using a USB connection, move content. 70

Create a backup on a computer 71

Data synchronization using a computer 72

On a PC... 73

USE OF MICROSD CARD OR USB FLASH DRIVE 73

What choices are there for storage on the Device?.. 74

For data storage and restoration, use Samsung Cloud. 74

AUTOMATIC REVERSAL... 75

Backup Your Data 75

Share with your Computer url for Windows 76

HOW TO COPY DATA FROM WINDOWS PHONE 77

Launch "Windows Explorer" or "File Explorer." 78

CHAPTER SIX 79

PHONE CALLS 79

Set Wi-Fi Calling on or Off on a Samsung Galaxy S23 79

MAKE A PHONE CALL 80

Call-in options 80

Employ Speed Dial 81

SET UP a conference call 82

Reject a call by text message instead 82

ANSWERING CALLS 83

Blocking Hidden Or Unknown Numbers 86

RINGTONES AND CALL NOTIFICATIONS 87

SETTING FOR QUICK DECLINE MESSAGES 88

VIDEO CALLS 89

Built-in video calling and chat 90

Video call on your PC 91

VIEW AND DELETE CALL HISTORY 91

How to access call records 92

Consult the voicemail menu 94

CHAPTER SEVEN 96

APPLICATION CONTACTS for S23 ULTRA 96

Create a contact 96

CHANGE OR ELIMINATE A CONTACT 97

INSERT A RINGTONE 97

MAKE A CONTACT BACKUP 98

EDITING CONTACTS 99

MANAGEMENT OF PHONE CONTACTS 99

Build Your Image 100

Manage duplicate contacts 101

Create a Group 102

    Block a contact 103

Controlling Contact Storage 103

CHAPTER EIGHT 105

MESSAGES 105

SENDING AN SOS MESSAGES IN S23 ULTRA 105

HOW TO READ MESSAGES I RECEIVED 110

    A message being sent 113

Sending an MMS 116

    Indicate when text messages have been read and delivered. 119

    Deletion of a message 123

    Message forwarding 125

    Message blocking 127

Using My Emoji to Send a Message 131

    Send a text by voice 134

CHAPTER NINE 136

PHONE SETTINGS 136

DARK MODE 136

Set the Night or Dark setting manually. 136

    Schedule the use of the Dark or Night modes. 137

Turn on the eye comfort screen. 138

    ADJUST BRIGHTNESS SETTING 139

    Elevate the brightness settings 139

CHANGE THE DISPLAY AND FONT OPTIONS 139

SCREEN TIMEOUT 140

FONT SIZE AND STYLE 142

Install a new font 143

Make use of high contrast fonts...144

CHAPTER TEN...145

SOUND AND VIBRATION SETTING ON S23 ULTRA..........................145

Customize noises, vibrations, and notifications 145

List of Galaxy phone sound settings 149

CHAPTER ELEVEN...151

CONNECTION SETUP...151

How to Connect a Samsung Galaxy Smartphone to a Smart Gadget...............153

How to Connect Several Devices Using Bluetooth 153

Finished media..153

Disable Bluetooth Pairing: How to Do It Upon completion of your work 153

Activate or deactivate NFC on the Samsung Galaxy S23 Ultra. 154

How to activate and deactivate Airplane Mode on S23 Ultra devices...............154

Longer Battery Life 154

ON/OFF SWITCH FOR THE AIRPLANE MODE 155

Using the Settings menu's Airplane mode...............................155

Triple Tap Connections 156

MOBILE NETWORK SETTING...156

DATA USAGE 160

Analyze data usage by app 161

MOBILE HOTSPOTS 164

Enable mobile hotspot..164

via Quick Settings..165

Set Up A Mobile Hotspot 165

Mobile hotspot timeout settings 166

CHAPTER TWENTY 167

LOCK SCREEN AND SECURITY 167

Where can I change how my devices operate?............................167

Install Biometric Security...169

Safe Lock Configurations 169

Time, Date, and Alarm 170

Date and time should be set. 170

Set a new time zone. 172

Setup an alarm. 172

On/Off the alarm switch 172

Eliminate an alarm 173

Using the Sleep mode. 174

CHAPTER THIRTEEN 177

BIOMETRICS AND SECURITY 177

Fingerprint Security. 177

How to sign up with your finger 178

For More Accurate Fingerprint Recognition 180

Use of fingerprint identification 181

Displaying The Fingerprint Icon 181

Erasing Recorded Fingerprints 182

If your phone doesn't detect your fingerprint right away 182

If accidentally vibrating or unlocking while attempting to scan a fingerprint ... 183

FACE IDENTIFICATION 183

Configure Facial Recognition 184

A word used in biometrics is facial recognition. 184

Facial detection alternatives 185

Tips on Face Recognition 186

DIGITAL WELLBEING 186

View The Apps Dashboard 186

Reduce Feature 189

PARENTAL CONTROL 190

Setup a Samsung account for your child. 191

Put parental controls in place 192

Give up monitoring an account 194

SET UP SAMSUNG PASS 195

Configure Samsung Pass. 195

Utilizing Samsung Pass.. 196

Activate and deactivate Autofill 197

Disable Samsung Pass. 198

Create A Secure Folder 199

Add applications or folders to the secure folder................................... 200

Hide the Secured Folder 202

Access methods for Secure Folder 203

Uninstall Secure Folder.. 204

CHAPTER FOURTEEN.. 205

GOOGLE APPLICATIONS.. 205

Make use of Google apps 205

Use Microsoft applications 206

CHAPTER FIFTEEN 208

APPLICATIONS USAGE... 208

Any independently purchased app may well be uninstalled................... 208

You can deactivate or uninstall applications from the apps screen................. 209

Through the settings menu, remove or deactivate apps. 211

Through the apps screen, remove or deactivate applications. 211

LATEST APPS DOWNLOAD 213

App update 215

Uninstall an application 215

Install the application again.. 215

CHAPTER SIXTEEN.. 216

SAMSUNG CAMERA ULTILIZATION 216

Night selfies and nighttime portraits... 216

A selfie video and a nighttime video 217

SHOOTING MODES 218

Set up the shooting modes.. 219

   Add and modify background effects for pictures in portrait mode. 220

CAMERA SETTINGS 220

Key Features 221

   Pictures 221

ALBUM CREATION 222

   WATCH AND EDIT MOVIES AND IMAGES. 222

   Create albums for your photos and videos. 223

Remove the photos and videos. 224

Album Creation.. 225

   BUILD A STANDARD ALBUM. 225

SORT ALBUMS INTO GROUPS 226

SHARE IMAGES AND VIDEOS. 226

TAKE TEXT OUT OF A VIDEO 227

CHAPTER SEVENTEEN 229

Gallery Settings... 229

How to control your Gallery app's photos and videos by syncing them with
OneDrive... 229

   How to link your MS and Samsung accounts using Cloud Sync........................ 229

   How to connect particular albums in the Gallery application 231

How to get documents off OneDrive................................ 233

How to retrieve deleted OneDrive data 234

   How to synchronize your Gallery photos and videos with OneDrive right away
.... 234

How to take a screenshot on the Samsung S23 Ultra 236

   METHOD 1: Volume Down + Power Keys 236

Method 2: Utilize a Palm Gesture to take a picture on a Samsung S23. 237

Greetings, Bixby!.. 238

Using the screen recorder on the Samsung smartphone...................................... 240

xi

Using Screen Recordings 241

Making use of your Quick Options 243

Making use of your Advanced Options... 244

CHAPTER EIGHTEEN 254

CALENDAR USAGE 254

Basic Calendar application navigation.. 254

Steps for setting up the calendar 255

How to change your calendar settings 255

How to create an event 256

How to modify or remove an event 257

How to sync your calendar with recently added external accounts 258

Calendar Sharing.. 258

CHAPTER NINETEEN 259

CALL MAKING WITH GOOGLE DUO 259

Before Beginning 259

Create A Group 259

Share a link to launch a conference session. 259

Call a current group or participate in a live group conversation..................... 260

Suspect Groups... 261

Get rid of a group member... 261

Tap to remove from group. 261

Utilize Google Duo to make contacts from other applications 261

Have various carriers: Call is made with Google Duplex. 261

What if the standard video calling tool is not the Duo app?............................ 263

Installing the Duo application... 263

GROUP VIDEO CALLS USING GOOGLE DUO... 264

CHAPTER TWENTY 266

NOTES AND FILES APPS.. 266

Functions and options for Samsung Notes.. 266

A variety of notes are displayed in Samsung Notes. 267

Importing and exporting data in Samsung Notes.............................. 269

Update Samsung Notes 269

Organize folders, templates, and note types. 270

Share your notes... 270

S PEN APPLICATION 272

Memos Written by Hand 272

ON IMAGES, ADD TEXT OR DRAWINGS. 274

Utilize Smart Select... 275

Open the S Pen's settings 275

Shortcuts for editing Air commands.. 276

Set Air view to on or off... 277

Merge the S Pen 278

Charge the S Pen... 279

S PEN REMOTE PREFERENCES OPTIONS.. 279

Use the S Pen Fold Edition... 280

CAPTURING A VIDEO TO GENERATE GIFs....................................... 281

Create a GIF image from a collection of images........................... 281

How to snap a burst of shots.. 282

Make a GIF right away by using the Camera app 283

CHAPTER TWENTY-ONE.. 284

HEALTH APP FOR SAMSUNG 284

Pair watch and phone together... 284

Download and install the Samsung Health Check program. 285

The Galaxy Wearable application has been updated. 286

CHAPTER TWENTY-TWO.. 288

SAMSUNG PAY 288

Use the application to pay using it 288

Use the cards you prefer to pay. 289

Make a transaction using a Galaxy watch 290

Make a payment using a gift card 290

Return your purchase 291

A purchase that cannot be reversed 291

How should I arrange the menu icons in my Samsung Wallet Quick Access? 292

Delete or add cards to the Quick Access group................................... 292

Quick access and default card 293

Order the Quick Access tab elements differently 293

With Samsung Pay, you can buy and use gift cards. 294

Make a gift card purchase for yourself... 294

Buy a friend a gift card... 296

Use a gift card to make a purchase 297

Internet payment... 297

CHAPTER TWENTY-THREE... 298

SAMSUNG DEX... 298

Adding a PC and mouse 299

How to make calls and send messages using other Galaxy devices.................. 299

Set up the "Call and text on other smartphones" feature. 300

How to use your smartphone to make calls.. 301

CHAPTER TWENTY-TWO.. 302

DIFFERENT TIPS AND TRCKS ON SAMSUNG GALAXY S23 ULTRA 302

Display advice 302

TIPS & TRICKS FOR NOTIFICATIONS.. 304

GAME-BOOSTING ADVICE 305

PHOTO AND CAMERA TIPS 306

Taking A Screenshot 308

TIPS FOR TAKING PHOTOS.. 309

INDEX 311

INTRODUCTION

Samsung Galaxy S23 Ultra

The Samsung Galaxy S23 Ultra is the top-of-the-line Android device for 2023, if that's what you're searching for. It is the only model in the S23 series to include the 200MP ISOCELL HP2 camera sensor, the 5,000mAh battery, and 1TB of storage, pushing the limits of what is possible with smartphones. The 6.8" Dynamic AMOLED 2x display, the only one in the series with adaptive refresh rates between 1 and 120Hz, should operate quickly and easily on the Qualcomm Snapdragon 8 Gen 2 Mobile Platform for Galaxy, and everything on it should appear lovely and smooth.

Design

Because the S Pen is only available on the Galaxy S23 Ultra, it has a squarer form factor than the rest of the line. Only barely curved, the back panel and display follow the side edges. The S23 Ultra is thinner than the previous Galaxy Note models.

The rear panel of the Galaxy S23 Ultra does not have a protruding camera housing. An alternative, cleaner, more minimalist design is achieved by placing each camera in its own spherical cutout. The face camera has an Infinity-O cutout in the display. The physical keys are on the right edge of the phone, and the bottom edge of the device has a speaker grille and USB-C port.

1

Phantom Black, Cream, Green, and Lavender are the four standard color choices that Samsung has prepared for the Galaxy S23 Ultra. For resilience to water and dust, the phone has IP68 certification. It weighs 234 grams and is 163.4 x 78.1 x 8.9mm in size.

Display

The 6.8-inch Quad HD+ (3088 x 1440) touchscreen on Samsung's 2023 flagship phone has an adjustable refresh rate of 1-120Hz.

The Dynamic AMOLED 2X screen is HDR10+ compatible. Gorilla Glass Victus 2 provides protection, which should improve impact resistance without reducing the glass's resistance to surface scratches.

The screen has the same 1750 nits of brightness as the 2022 model, but thanks to Vision Booster technology, it has excellent color accuracy and enhanced outdoor visibility. In game mode, the screen also features a 240Hz touch sampling rate.

Specifications

The Qualcomm-Exynos duality could be eliminated with the Galaxy S23 Ultra's inclusion of a Snapdragon chipset in every region. The Snapdragon 8 Gen 2 chipset, which was produced on a 4nm node, powers the latest flagship.

Furthermore, the Galaxy S23 Ultra is equipped with a special Snapdragon 8 Gen 2 chip that has marginally faster CPU and GPU clock rates.

Other hardware specifications include 256GB, 512GB, or 1TB of UFS 4.0 storage, as well as 8/12GB of LPPDR5 Memory.

Support is provided for GPS, GLONASS, BeiDou, and Galileo. The device accepts one **eSIM** and has two physical SIM slots. Its 5,000mAh battery can be charged quickly at 45W. Wi-Fi 6e, Bluetooth 5.3, and 5G are tools for connectivity.

Camera

The 200MP main camera on the Galaxy S23 Ultra is a first for a Samsung flagship device. The f/1.7 lens, 85-degree field of view, and enhanced image stabilization are all present. The new **ISOCELL HP2** sensor, which was unveiled in January 2023, is the basis for the camera. In addition to 200MP image capture, it also offers 12.5MP and 50MP modes using 4-in-1 and 16-in-1 pixel binning, respectively.

Without much cropping, the camera can record 8K 30fps videos and boasts enhanced low-light autofocus due to Super Quad Phase Detection. The photographer can record 4K 60fps HDR videos while concurrently taking 12.5MP photos with Smart ISO Pro.

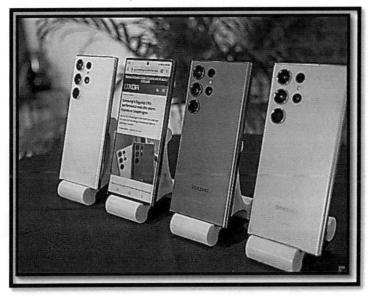

SAMSUNG GALAXY S PEN

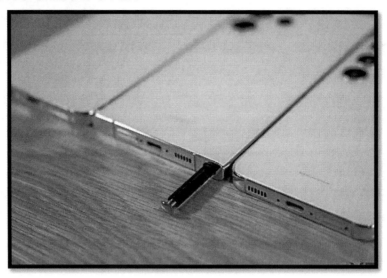

Last but not least, the Samsung Galaxy S23 Ultra includes an incorporated S Pen, exactly like the model from a year ago, which was the first time the S23 series and the Note range were combined. The **S Pen** docks in a silo in the lower right corner and waits until you're ready to use it before moving into view.

CHAPTER ONE

INSERTING THE SIM/ MICRO AND NANO

INSERT / REMOVE SIM CARD

Never try to put the SIM card in while the gadget is turned on. The SIM card and/or the gadget could be damaged if you do this.

Make sure the machine is turned off.

- An ejector Passcode for you was packaged with your new device. Put a light push into the SIM tray's pinhole. The switch will turn on.

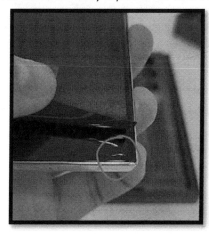

Check the container, please. In the image below, the dual SIM slot lets you use either two SIM cards or one SIM card and an SD card.

- Your SIM tray might look different depending on your model, but by examining the marks and symbols on the tray, you can determine where each card fits. A memory card or two SIM cards are not supported by all devices.

- Place the memory card or SIM in the tray with the metal contacts downward.

Note: If your SIM card is the wrong dimension for your SIM tray, you should get additional assistance from your network provider.

- Carefully reinstall the plate in your device. It should rest flush against your device if you position it correctly.

REMOVING A SIM OR MEMORY CARD

You should unmount the memory card before removing it in order to prevent any harm or data loss. Not required when getting a SIM device.

How to Remove an SD Card

- Click Settings, then choose Maintenance or Device maintenance.
- Click Capacity
- Touch SD Card

NOTE: By clicking the More choices button, which resembles three dots, you can choose this option if it is not visible. Select Storage choices next. You should be able to touch the SD card at this point.

- Select Mount

The SIM or memory card should then be taken out of the slot. In order to insert a SIM or memory card in a device with a removable battery, follow the instructions there.

POWERING ON/OFF THE DEVICE

To quickly switch off the Samsung Galaxy S23, press and hold the side button and the volume down button simultaneously (previously called the power button).

The Galaxy S23 ultra can be turned off using the collection of buttons.

The process of turning off a phone has curiously complicated over the past few years. There are some situations where you can't just press the power button to switch off a phone; instead, modern phones will launch Google Assistant or Bixby instead. The change is not limited to Samsung Galaxy phones. On smartphones operating Android 12 and later, manufacturers have the choice to wake the virtual assistant instead of bringing up the power menu. In this circumstance, manufacturers frequently renamed the "Power off" button to "Side button" to represent the change.

You can quickly switch off your Samsung Galaxy S23 ultra by following these simple steps.

Locate the side and volume-down buttons:

• The volume button is the large one on the right edge of the phone (when the screen is facing you). The volume down button is located on the bottom part of this long button.

• The side button is the tiny button that sits beneath the bigger volume button.

• Squeeze them together and hold for three to five seconds. It will open the power options on your screen.

• Click the Power off or Restart buttons on the screen to switch the device off or restart it.

• Quickly clicking the volume Down and side buttons will capture a screenshot.

If you accidentally activated the power menu rather than taking a screenshot, release the buttons and try again, keeping them pressed together for an extended period of time. Navigating the side key will give you access to the power option.

Thankfully, it's relatively simple to go back to the previous behavior, in which clicking the side key opened the power menu.

Following are the steps:

- Under Settings > Advanced Functions, select Side key.
- Select the Power off menu choice in the Push and Hold region.
- By doing this, the Power off menu choice rather than the default Wake Bixby option will be chosen.

- If you hold down the Side key for a lengthy time, your Galaxy S23 will now launch the power menu.

Making use of the Quick Settings menu.

If you don't want to memorize the button combination, you can use the helpful power menu shortcut that Samsung's One UI skin has included in the Quick Settings menu.

- ➤ To access the notification shade, swipe down once on your home screen.
- ➤ To access the Quick Settings menu, swipe down once more.
- ➤ A power icon may be found in the top right corner of the screen, between the search icon (a magnifying glass) and the settings icon (a cogwheel).
- ➤ The power menu will be accessible by tapping the power icon.
- ➤ Bixby may be used to switch off a phone.

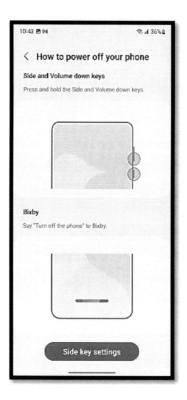

- ❖ Your Samsung Galaxy S23 ultra can also be turned off for you via the Bixby speech assistant.
- ❖ By tapping the Side key or saying "Hello Bixby," you can get Bixby to wake up.
- ❖ Speak the phrases "Switch off," "Turn off," or "Restart my phone."

As soon as Bixby comprehends what you said, a confirmation page with two buttons for powering down and restarting will appear. Following your selection of the preferred option, the phone will respond appropriately.

Forcefully restart a stalled Galaxy S23 Ultra

If your Samsung Galaxy S23 ultra is unresponsive, it will be difficult to begin any of the aforementioned procedures.

- In this case, it is possible to compel the device to restart.
- Discover the side and volume down buttons.
- Hold them there for about 15 seconds while you squeeze them together.

- Your phone's display will turn off after a brief vibration.
- The Splashscreen and boot animation that follow this serve as confirmation of a successful force restart.
- Your phone will soon start up again and bring you to the Home Screen as normal.
- If restarting your phone by force puts you in a Bootloop, where you repeatedly loop back to the splash screen and boot animation without ever reaching the Home Screen, your phone requires further troubleshooting.

USING THE QUICK SETTING PANEL

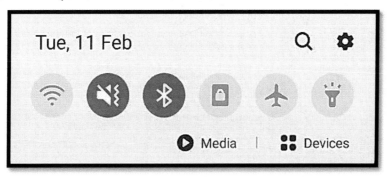

There are a ton of helpful settings and features on your Galaxy device, but it can be difficult to locate them fast. The Fast Settings menu allows you to access what you need without opening the settings program. By using the Quick Settings interface, you can, for instance, use the torch, mirror your phone's screen to your TV, or instantly turn off Wi-Fi. Even the Quick Settings panel can be altered so that your most frequently used choices are always close at hand.

- The Quick Settings window is opened
- The Quick Settings panel is concealed above the Notification Tray.
- You can choose to access the Quick Settings panel in its entirety or just your favorite Quick Settings.
- Opening the Quick Options, which you use most frequently

1. Swipe down from the top of the screen to reveal your notifications.

2 Your Quick Settings are located directly above the notification tray.

3 To access all of your Quick Settings, once more swipe down from the top of the screen.

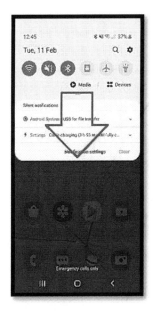

Making use of the Quick Settings

Your most frequently used functions can be rapidly turned on and off using the Fast Settings panel. It can also be used to enter the settings app or rapidly alter a feature's settings.

1 To access your Quick Settings, swipe down from two points at the top of the screen.

2.To activate or deactivate a feature, tap on it. When the button turns blue, it is on.

3 To show more possibilities, swipe left.

4 To modify settings, tap the feature's name.

5 Certain options will be grayed out if the feature is disabled. Switch on the function to gain access to more choices.

6.Only a few of the most popular features will be displayed to you in the Quick Settings window. Tap Details to view all of the feature's setup options.

7.You will be directed to the feature's comprehensive settings page.

Rearrange the button location.

You can reorder the buttons in the Quick Settings panel to make it even easier to reach the settings you use the most frequently. The first six icons are noticeable when the notification tray is opened.

1. Swipe from two locations on the top of the screen downward to reach your Quick Settings.

2. Three dots will show up when you select the options icon.

3 Tap Button Order; alternatively, it may appear as Edit Buttons on some smartphones.

4.To reorder the buttons, hold down and drag them. The notification tray will open with the first six buttons visible.

5 Drag buttons that you don't frequently use to the top of the screen to remove them from the Quick Settings panel. These may always be dragged back onto the Quick Settings window in the future.

6 Tap Reset to restore the button order to its original state.

7 Tap Done when you're satisfied with the sequence of your buttons.

19

Flight mode

Flight mode has several benefits beyond merely traveling. Flight mode is the quickest method to quickly disable your Bluetooth, Wi-Fi, and mobile network connections with a single tap. This makes it incredibly convenient for all of those moments when you don't want to be interrupted or receive a notification.

1 To access your Quick Settings, swipe downward from two points at the top of the screen.

2.To activate or deactivate the feature, tap the flying mode button. The feature will be operational when the button turns blue.

MAKING USE OF THE SIDE AND VOLUME KEYS

The volume Key

The primary function of the **volume key** is to change the loudness. The two buttons are **Volume Up and Volume Down,** respectively.

➤ On Android smartphones like the Galaxy S23 ultra, the volume key can be used for extra functions.

➤ The Galaxy S23 Ultra camera software, for example, may use the volume key as a shutter button when the on-screen shutter button is difficult to use. On the Galaxy S23 ultra, you can capture by simultaneously holding the Volume Down key and the Side key.

➤ If the Galaxy S23 ultra hangs, you might also need to press the volume key to compel (rather than softly) restart it.

➤ Beginning with the Galaxy S20, Samsung shifted the volume key to the right edge of the device (same as iPhone by chance, lol).

➤ When you press the volume key on the Galaxy S23 ultra, the volume slider will immediately show if no media is being played.

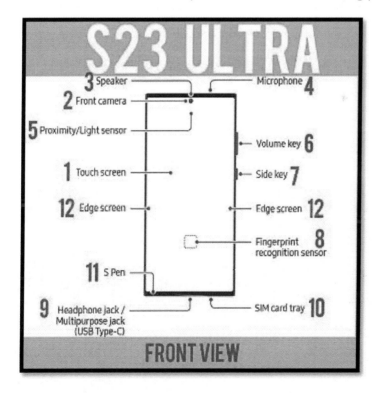

Side key

The Side key can be used to turn **on** or **off** the Galaxy S23 Ultra.

For instance, when you first obtain a Galaxy S23, you always press the Side key for a few seconds to start the phone and set it up. It can also be used to open the Power-off menu or to start Bixby.

The Side key's most popular use is to turn off the screen (and after that lock the phone).

With the Galaxy S23 ultra, the Camera app can also be opened by pressing the Side key without first unlocking the device.

GPS Antenna

While looking at the phone from the screen, the GPS antenna is situated on the opposite side of the camera from the top left corner.

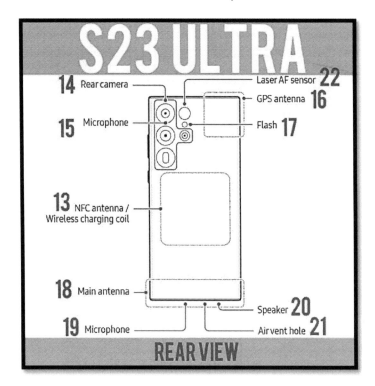

CHAPTER TWO

SAMSUNG GALAXY S23 ULTRA SETUP

This is the ultimate manual for comprehending all of the features of the Galaxy S23 Ultra.

How to restart or switch off the Samsung Galaxy S23 ultra

Samsung's Bixby speech assistant is by default activated by the ultra-right-side button on the S23. The lock page appears after only a short press of the button. You must concurrently press and hold the power button and the volume down key to turn the device off (not briefly, as doing so will only take a snapshot). When you do this, a software menu with the choices "Switch off," "Restart," and "Emergency mode" will appear. Additionally, you can modify the "Side key settings" option on this page to make a long press open the power menu rather than Bixby.

THE HOME SCREEN

Switch on gesture control. Button settings are still available from Samsung, and they might be enabled by default.

> ➤ To change to Android motions, navigate to settings > display > navigation bar.

➢ From here, you can alter the button order, or you can select "Swipe gestures" in its stead.

Create a new main screen:

By long pressing any home page, the wallpaper, style, themes, widgets, and other options can all be changed. Alternatively, you can delete all of the screens here by tapping the enormous plus sign in a circle after swiping to a new tab (hit the trash can icon up top).

Your UI's colours should be changed:

Materials for Android The options on the home screen will take you to the function. Next, pick a design and a wallpaper. In addition to changing the backgrounds from the default settings, which include animated "video" options, you can select a color scheme in this area. You can then change the user interface's color scheme to fit your wall decor. The option to apply it to icons is also available, but it only functions with folder backgrounds or native Samsung applications.

Increase the size of the main screen's content:

You can customize the grid size on which your shortcuts and widgets are displayed based on how crowded you want your home page to be. Long-press the main screen, then select "Settings" by swiping up from the bottom right. You can customize the home page and/or the applications tray using the settings for 4x5, 4x6, and 5x5, 5x6.

How to access Google Discover:

Simply swipe from left to right across the home page. If you favor Samsung's alternative, long-press on the home screen and swipe right to access the left-hand page. Use the toggle at the top to fully disable this page, or choose between Google Explore or Samsung Free here.

Instructions for changing a widget:

Long-press the home screen and select "Widgets" to view widgets. A widget must be added to the home page or any subsequent pages before you can make any adjustments to them. Simply press and hold any widget after it has been placed to show a border with four circular "pull points."

Stack widgets:

You can group widgets together into a "stack" that you can swipe across to view data from a variety of sources, as opposed to having each widget displayed separately. By pressing and keeping any widget, you can "make stack" and "add more widgets to that stack.".

percent of the display power You can change it on or off by choosing the "Display battery percentage" option under Settings > Notifications > Advanced Settings.

Landscape mode is permitted on your main page:

This option allows you to show the home page, applications tray, settings, and other screens in landscape mode. By selecting "Rotate to landscape view" under settings > home screen settings, you can turn it on even though it is disabled by default.

Drag apps onto one another on any page of the main screen or in the app trays to create folders. A pop-up menu with the opportunity to remove or uninstall the program will show when you open a folder and long-press an app. Applications that let you select multiples from your list can be added by dragging them into the folder or by clicking the "+" icon inside the folder.

Open the folder and type the new name at the top to change a folder's name or hue. If you don't want a name to show, leave it blank; nothing will.

By clicking the dot in the top right corner and selecting a different color, including entirely unique alternatives, the folder backdrop color can be changed individually for each folder.

Removing a section Hold down the button while choosing the garbage can icon to delete a folder. Upon your request, the apps' folder and links will vanish, but the apps themselves won't be removed.

If you don't want certain apps to show up in searches or on your home page, you can hide them. To hide apps, long-press the main screen, select Settings, "Hide apps," then "Done" after selecting the ones you don't want to appear. A word of caution: Searching occasionally still yields the app's options.

AVAILABILITY OF CONNECTIONS

A brand-new menu item called "connected devices" presents a variety of choices.

How to Configure eSIM

You will have the chance to configure eSIM if it is enabled during the original setup of your device.

 ➢ After initial configuration, make the adjustment by going to settings > connections > SIM management > add eSIM.

Utilizing Samsung DeX

The desktop experience (DeX) feature on the Galaxy S23 ultra allows you to use your phone as a desktop computer by connecting it to a PC, a TV, or a monitor.

 ➢ By going to settings > linked devices, you can view DeX.
 ➢ Use the bottom USB-C port on the monitor to link your phone to the Samsung DeX app, or download it to your computer and operate it there in a window.
 ➢ Additionally, it will function with USB-C devices.

Note: To avoid frequently switching between them while working, you can use your Samsung account to enable calls and texts to be accepted on other Samsung devices, such as a tablet.

- ➢ Go to settings > linked devices > call & SMS on other devices to enable it.
- ➢ This implies that texts and phone conversations to the number on your phone will be synchronized across all of your Samsung devices.

Link to Windows

By connecting to a Windows Computer, you can manage mobile notifications, view recent photos, make and take calls from a Windows PC, read messages and conversations, and sync mobile apps.

- ➢ Go to settings > connected devices > Connect to Windows to turn it on. You will then be led through the setup process.

You can personalize Android Auto on Samsung devices

- ➢ On Samsung phones, the Android Auto user experience is customizable.
- ➢ Navigate to settings > Linked Devices to enable Android Auto.
- ➢ You can change a few other settings and the applications that Android Auto shows you here.

The screen of your phone can be projected onto a separate device, like a TV, using Smart View.

- ➢ Go to settings > connected devices to activate Smart View.
- ➢ As a consequence, you can mirror on an appropriate device.
- ➢ You can reverse the process with some gadgets that can be mirrored on your Samsung phone.

Utilizing Digital Assistants

Bixby is marketed by Samsung as the brand's default digital helper. Google Assistant is also available on the S23 ultra because it uses Android. That option also becomes accessible once Amazon Alexa is installed. The management options for each of these virtual assistants are outlined below.

Using Google Assistant, the virtual on-screen softkey can be used to launch Google Assistant by giving it a long press. If you're using gestures, a 45-degree corner swipe will trigger the same. This syncs with your Google account and is compatible with all of your Google Assistant preferences as soon as you log in.

The hot-word "Hey/Ok Google" is available in the Google app and will cause Google to only respond verbally. If you did not enable this during initial setup, the quickest way to access the settings is to launch Google Assistant (as explained above) and say "show me Google Assistant settings." By choosing it as the first choice in the settings menu, Hello Google and Voice Match can be enabled.

WAYS TO DISABLE GOOGLE ASSISTANT

You can turn off Google Assistant or any other helper if you don't want one.

> ➢ Under Settings > Apps > Choose Default Apps, select "Digital helper app" and "Device assistance app."

➤ You can select "None" or another option if you want to disable the preset system.

You can change your personal assistant: Install the Alexa app, and if you'd like, change the usual device assistance app to Bixby Voice or Alexa in accordance with the advice above. As a result, you will be able to launch Alexa from the center button. However, the hot-word for Alexa won't work.

App Tips

All apps should be visible on the home screen: This setting is preferred by some users. You can eliminate the applications tray by long-pressing the home screen and choosing settings. Next, select "Home screen alone" from the "Home screen arrangement" menu.

Apps menu buttons can be added or removed: By default, there is no button to press to access the apps tray; instead, you must swipe. If you want the icon back, go to the home screen settings as previously mentioned and select the "Display applications screen button on home screen" toggle.

Apps can be sorted sequentially or according to preferences: While in the applications tray, hit the triple-dot menu in the top-right search bar of the Finder and select "Sort" from the drop-down menu. After that, you can select alphabetical sequence.

Choose "Custom order" if you'd like, and then drag your apps into the places you want.

Create a tray area for your apps: You can have a folder for holding multiple applications, regardless of how your apps tray is set up—custom or alphabetically. Simply tap and hold one program icon while dragging it over another, and the apps tray will immediately create a folder. Just like on the home screens, you can then alter the name and color.

Allow Finder to propose some apps to you: You will instantly get suggestions based on recently used apps when you hit the Finder (search bar) at the top of the apps tray. Choose the triple-dot menu to disable the suggested apps, search suggestions, suggested settings, downloads & screenshots, search history, and hidden apps if you don't want this.

App Removal: You can remove an app by clicking on its icon. You can delete the app by just long pressing it; a pop-up menu will appear. The same option will allow you to disable an app if it's a core program (which you cannot delete).

Adding applications to your home screen in the apps tray, click and hold the app shortcut. From the pop-up option that opens, you can choose "add to home."

Prevent new app icons from being added to the home screen: You can discover the "Add new apps to home screen" toggle by going into the home screen settings (long-pressing the wallpaper and selecting the settings cog).

By default, it is off, however enabling it will make every new install visible on your home screens.

If you have multiple apps that can perform the same function, Android lets you choose which one should be the default. Choose the default apps under Settings > Apps. Options include browser, caller ID/spam filtering, assistant, home, phone, and SMS.

Manage app permissions: Android enables you to individually control each app's permissions. Choose the desired app by going to Settings > Apps and clicking Permissions. You can use this to turn off access to your contacts' information or location, for example. But, keep in mind that doing so can result in a limited functionality or a persistent request for permission from an app.

Enhance your video calls by adding effects, such as changing the background color or image, to them. Common apps like Meet, Zoom, and WhatsApp are compatible with this. Go to settings > advanced features > video call effects to see the option. Once configured, a camera effects icon will show up during calls, allowing you to turn it on or off.

Lock screen as well as always display

You will see the lock page when your phone is locked. The actual lock screen is divided into two sections: one when the screen is off, where "always-on display" can give you some information, and another when the screen is completely on but you can't access the device.

Turn on the permanent display: To have the screen continuously show information, go to settings > lock screen and toggle **on "Always On Display."** You can choose to show on demand, only when new alerts are received, or always by selecting this option. Just bear in mind that having your smartphone light up constantly can reduce its lifespan because it consumes energy.

Change the look of the always-on clock: The always-on display on the S23 ultra has a selection of calendar designs. Go to settings > lock screen > always on show to modify the clock style. The clock's style, including "Image clocks," can be selected, and the colors can be changed.

Samsung products allow you to add widgets to your lock screen or always-on display.

If not, go to settings > lock screen > widgets. An audio controller probably already exists there by default. Every feature, including routines, the speech recorder, the weather, alarms, and more, can be turned on and off from this page.

The brightness of the always-on monitor can be changed: This is connected to your phone's auto brightness, but you can actively override it. Select Always-On Display in the Lock Screen section of Preferences.

This menu's 'Auto brightness' option can be discovered. You can specifically regulate the brightness of the always-on display by turning this off. You can directly change the brightness by double touching the always-on display once it is visible.

Alternative options for the lock screen: For quick entry, there are two shortcuts on the lock screen (only the lock screen, not the always-on display). They can be any program, but by default they are the phone and camera. Make your adjustments by tapping the lock screen diagram under settings > lock screen. Here, you can deactivate the left and right shortcuts completely or choose to use them.

Settings for lock screen notifications: To activate or disable lock screen, navigate to settings > notifications > lock screen notification. You can decide whether notifications show on the always-on display, complete details, content, and icon-only display. The background and text transparency of the message can also be altered using a slider.

If the local time is shown while you are traveling but you also want to see your home time, go to options > lock screen > roaming clock. This will make a moving clock appear on the lock screen. Additionally, you have control over how your local time zone is determined and can modify it as necessary.

Security and unlocking

The best security advice is to never use biometrics to access your smartphone; instead, always use a password or PIN. Your device's security depends entirely on the passcode or PIN you use, as anyone wishing to hack into your phone can always choose to do so.

Make face or fingerprint protection active: To turn on fingerprint or face protection, go to settings > security and privacy > biometrics. You can sign up here with your visage or fingerprints (or multiple prints). You'll need to concurrently establish a backup PIN or password to increase security. If you're using a fingerprint to open your phone, it's best to register fingers from both hands so you can do so regardless of how you're holding the device.

Swift lock: When you press the standby button, you want your phone to immediately secure. Select lock screen from the settings menu, then safeguard lock settings. You have the option to lock the device when you press the standby button or the screen goes to slumber. If you do want a time delay, there are lots of options available.

Automate the gadget wipe: You can cause a factory reset on your phone, which would delete all of your apps and data, after 20 unsuccessful efforts to unlock it, even though this is not a setting we would generally recommend using. You can find the same Secure lock settings here as in the aforementioned recommendation.

Characteristics of the lock network and security: You won't be able to modify your network settings while your phone is locked if you use this choice. This will make it easier to recover your phone if it is taken. However, it also implies that in order to activate flight mode, you must first unlock your phone. Go to settings > lock screen > secure lock settings to locate the toggle to turn it on or off.

If you're worried that someone might access your phone and find information they shouldn't, keep your private files and apps in the Secure Folder. After this adds an additional layer of security, you can add files, pictures, and apps that you want to keep private, like personal or business data. Any software you want to use secretly and securely can have a second edition added. Under settings > security and privacy, you can find the private folder.

DO NOT DISTURB, VOLUME CONTROLS, AND SOUND

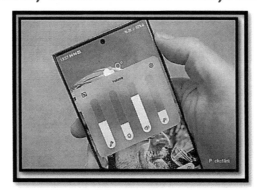

Learn how to adjust the media volume

- Go to Settings > Sounds and Vibrations > Volume to access the "Use Volume Keys for Media" choice.
- Because this option is turned on by default, only the media volume, such as your music, changes when you press the volume buttons.
- It controls the ringer level when it is off, but it switches to the media volume when media is being played, like through Netflix or Spotify.

Change the overall vibration intensities

- By going to settings > sounds and vibration > vibration intensity, you can separately change the vibration levels for calls, notifications, and touch input.
- Samsung wants your Galaxy to vibrate and beep with every contact and action, so turn off the keyboard, charging, and unlocking noises.
- By heading to settings > sound and vibration > system sounds/vibration control, you can turn them off.
- Go to settings > sounds and vibration > sound quality and effects to enable or disable Dolby Atmos, or select quick options.
- When you click into the Dolby Atmos section, you can select between separate upgrades for auto, movie, music, or speech.
- By activating a distinct "Dolby Atmos for gaming" toggle before accessing this menu, you can simply have Dolby Atmos launch whenever a game does.
- Adjust the EQ if you don't like the preset sound profile (equalizer). It is modifiable. Under settings > sounds and vibration > music quality and effects, type equalizer.

To adjust the sound profile as you see appropriate, you can switch between nine linear bands, five presets, and one custom setting (from 63Hz to 16kHz).

Utilize Convert music to alter the sound output

✓ Select Sounds and vibration > Sound quality and effects > Adapt Sound to open the settings window.
✓ This offers frequency enhancements based on age, according to the theory that some frequency bands are lowered in certain age categories.
✓ Use "Test my hearing" to decide which boost to use.

Do not bother mode: You can mute your phone using this Android function, but you can also create a number of exceptions. Swipe down to the fast settings section, then touch the do not disturb option to turn it on.

Additionally, you can hold down the button to schedule specific interruptions from calls, alarms, apps, and other sources.

✓ Go to settings > notifications > do not disturb to view this as well.
✓ As suggested earlier, allow alarms and exceptions in "do not disturb" zones.

Enable "do not disturb" option for notifications

Silent notifications are still possible even when vibrations and noises are muted.

✓ To hide notifications, go to Preferences > Notifications > Do Not Disturb.
✓ Using the controls below, you can choose whether to show or remove status bar icons, full-screen notifications, app icon badges, display in the notification panel, or any other type of message.
✓ Samsung has unique methods for configuring slumber mode.
✓ Samsung has unique methods for configuring sleep mode. Routines in settings. There are options here, including sleeping. You can use this to activate features that will help you set your phone down before bed, such as do not disturb and grayscale display changes.

RECOMMENDED BATTERIES

The brightness of the monitor should be decreased because it uses the most battery, which is not surprising. You can reach the notification shade and change the brightness by swiping downward.

✓ Change the resolution; a better resolution will result in a greater battery drain.

✓ However, you can find the option by going to settings > display, even though the directions are higher on the page.

Set all of your gadgets to "dark mode": The amount of electricity the phone needs to illuminate all of those white backgrounds is lessened, according to some evidence, when this is done. Once more, you can locate it in the display settings.

Stop using tools you don't need: Although Samsung phones have a ton of features, you won't use them. Usually, you can switch them off. All of the components for Bixby, NFC, the second SIM card port, edge panels, edge illumination, all vibration alerts, etc. may be included in that.

Check out what's using the battery: Navigate to Settings > Battery and Device Care. Toggle to "Battery."

❖ To see which applications have been utilizing the most battery life, scroll down.

❖ There may be some background surprises here, in which case you can search for them in the app settings to turn off particular rights or background activity.

❖ By choosing "last 7 days" from the battery usage screen depicted above, you can view your battery usage history.

❖ You can scroll down the page to see the applications that used the most battery the previous week.

❖ Some of these applications might surprise you, while others might just be a reflection of your usage habits.

❖ To enable power saving mode, use the shortcut in quick settings or go to settings > battery and device care > battery.

You can enable power-saving mode and choose the actions that will be done to protect your battery from damage here. It will limit motion smoothness, background network utilization, location access, and syncing to 60Hz.

Additionally, separate user-selectable options are available to turn off 5G connectivity, lower the CPU speed to 70%, decrease brightness by 10%, and disable the always-on display.

The leftover charge time is displayed when plugged into a charger. Look at the foot of the lock-screen and the battery status screen. It will show how much time is remaining and whether or not you are fast charging.

CHAPTER THREE

SAMSUNG ACCOUNT CREATION

Configuring an account in Setting

Software for Samsung accounts is available in the settings of Galaxy smartphones and devices.

- ❖ From the menu, select Preferences > Accounts and Backup.
- ❖ Under Manage Accounts > Upload Account, select Samsung Account.
- ❖ If you already have an account, log in by clicking or pressing this button. Create an account to make a new one.

- ❖ Tap Agree after reviewing the legal information.
- ❖ Complete the form and choose Establish account.

Your Samsung account management

The 2-step verification tool, which was recently implemented to improve the security of your Samsung account, can be used to rapidly sync your

Samsung account after it has been created or to verify your identity. Follow these steps to enter your registered Samsung account.

- From the menu, select Preferences > Accounts and Backup.
- Select Accounts.
- Tap the relevant Samsung account.

Establishing Two-Step Authentication

- Select Settings > Accounts and Restore from the menu.
- Choose Manage profiles and then choose the Samsung account you want to use.
- Click My Profile > Security Settings and select Two-Step Verification.

How to customize your content in Samsung services and applications

Step 1: Choose Settings > Accounts & Backup from the menu.

Step 2: Select Manage Accounts and then select the Samsung account that is registered.

Step 3: Choose Samsung Apps.

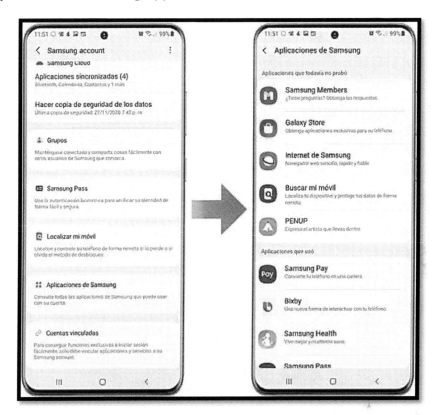

Note: Depending on the wireless service provider, software version, and device, different screens and settings might be available.

You can ask us a question through the Samsung Members app if you see odd activity on Samsung smartphones, tablets, or portable devices.

This enables us to examine the situation more closely. Only the duration of the investigation is retained on the anonymous data. Check out "How to use the Samsung Members app" for additional information on filing a bug report.

CHAPTER FOUR

HOME SCREEN AND APP DRAWER

Your phone and computer are no different from the rest of us; we all like to live in comfortable, spotless homes. By including widgets, folders, and extra Home Screens, as well as by reversing the screen's orientation, you can style and personalize your Home Screen. As a result, your gadget will become easier to use and more organized.

Note: Different screens and options might be available depending on the wireless service provider, software version, and type of device.

View of the Home Screen in nature

Keep in mind that not every device may enable this feature.

The default option on Galaxy smartphones is Auto rotate, which causes the device to change its display mode based on how you are holding it.

You can also lock the screen in landscape orientation if required. To reach the Quick settings menu, simply flip your iPhone over and swipe downward from the top of the screen. When you select Auto rotate, the device will now be locked in Landscape orientation. To get back to Auto rotate, simply select Landscape in the Quick settings panel.

Do you want to switch to landscape view on your home screen as well? To do this, go to Settings, pick Home Screen, and from the menu that pops up, choose Rotate to landscape view.

On the Quick settings panel, Auto rotate is turned on.

If you'd prefer, you may also set your Always On Display to appear in landscape mode. Tap Lock screen, then tap Always On Display from the Settings menu. Then select Landscape from the Screen orientation menu. All future displays of your AOD will be in landscape orientation.

Manage Home screens

- ❖ You want to access the important information as soon as you open your device, and the Home Screen is where you should start.
- ❖ Your Home screens can be configured however you like. You can add, remove, or modify your primary Home Screen to get it exactly how you want it.
- ❖ Touch and hold a blank area on any Home Screen.
- ❖ The display will switch to Edit mode and show numerous screens. Use these choices to manage your screens from here:

Control Wallpaper
- ➢ Change the wallpaper to further personalize your device's Home Screen.
- ➢ Choose one that is already loaded or a photo from your Gallery.

➢ On the Home screen, press and hold an empty area, then select Wallpaper and style.

➢ Also, you can go to Settings and select Wallpaper and style.

➢ To choose from preloaded wallpapers, hit Browse my wallpapers; to choose a specific photo, press Gallery.

Note: If you pick Gallery, you must first choose a photo before tapping Done.

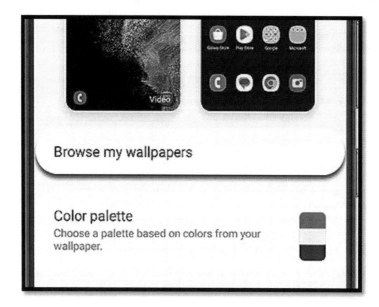

➢ Choose whether you want a certain wallpaper to appear on your lock screen, home screen, or both screens by tapping it.

➢ To view the wallpaper, select Preview.

➢ To install the wallpaper, select Done.

ADD OR REMOVE FOLDERS

➢ To keep all of your related programs in one location, your device comes preconfigured with folders like the Samsung folder.

➢ To assist you in organizing your other programs, you can also make and edit your own folders.

➢ Touch and hold an app on the Home Screen.

➢ To enter the Apps screen and select an app, you can alternatively slide up.

➢ Release after dragging the app over another app. The same folder will house both of the programs.
➢ Tap Folder name, then give the folder a suitable name.
➢ Hit the keyboard key for Done.

➢ Tap the Palette icon (the circle) in the top right corner to choose a color for the folder.
➢ By selecting Add (the plus sign), you can add new programs to the folder. You can also drag additional apps into the folder.
➢ Tap anywhere outside the folder to leave it.
➢ You can relocate the folder to a different location if it's currently on your Home Screen.
➢ Drag the folder to the desired location by touching and holding it.
➢ You may also tap and drag your folder if it's on the Applications screen to move it.
➢ Alternatively, you can press and hold the folder while selecting Add to Home.
➢ On the Home screen, a shortcut to the folder will display, and a copy of the folder will stay on the Apps screen.
➢ Touch and hold the chosen folder, then hit Delete to erase it.
➢ The apps will reappear on the Apps screen after the folder is deleted.

You will need to delete each instance of the same folder separately if you have more than one (for example, one on the Home Screen and one in Applications).

DELETE OR ADD WIDGETS

Widgets resemble scaled-down versions of programs.

- They show up on your Home Screen and when you tap them, an app function is activated or used.
- You can use these shortcuts to open your favorite programs more quickly.
- Swipe to a Home screen to add a widget. Next, touch and hold a free space.
- Choose the widget you want by tapping Widgets, and then hit Add.

- Just touch and hold a widget on the Home Screen, then select Remove to remove it.
- On your Home Screen, you may also arrange widgets into a stack.
- Create a widget first, then tap, hold, and release it.
- The widget you want to stack should first be selected by tapping Create stack.
- Hit Add.

The widgets can then be changed by swiping left and right.

- Touch and hold the selected widget stack to edit it.
- To delete a widget, touch Edit stack, then tap Delete (the minus icon) above the widget in question.
- Instead, select a new widget to add to the stack by tapping Add (the plus symbol).
- Also, you can tap the button next to the Auto rotate widgets.
- Your widgets will automatically rotate to display the most pertinent information if you do this.
- Touch and hold the widget stack you want to remove fully, hit Remove all, and then tap Remove when prompted.
- After you've put your widget in place, you have a few choices. You should be aware that the options can change depending on the widget.

Resize: Widgets with a blue border around their edges are resizable. By touching and dragging the lines, you can change its size.

Color: Change the color of your widget. By touching and holding the widget and tapping Settings, you can get to this.

Transparency: Change the widget's transparency to make it easier to see. By pressing and holding the widget and clicking Settings, you can get to this.

Replace the apps in the section of your preferred apps.
Your preferred app shortcuts will always be located in the bottom row on your Home Screen.

- If you want to change the layout of your Home Screen, you can remove these shortcuts and add new ones.
- These shortcuts can also be found in the taskbar of your One UI 5 Z Fold phone.
- Touch and hold the app shortcut from the Home Screen that you want to change or remove.

Then drag it to a different location on the screen. You can also select Remove to take the shortcut off your Home Screen. The Applications screen will still let you access the app.

Swipe up from the bottom of the screen to access the Apps page, where you may add a new favorite app shortcut. Drag the selected app to an open space next to the rest of your favorites by touching and holding it first.

This procedure can be repeated for each of your current favorites.

How to use smart search to replace the applications drawer on your Galaxy tablet

Unquestionably, one of the most recognizable aspects of Android OS is the applications drawer, which is also present in Samsung's One UI layer. It can be disabled, but from the standpoint of how the majority of users of Galaxy (Android) smartphones use their handsets, it makes little sense to do so.

Most tablets have displays big enough to accommodate all the apps you need on a single home screen, and the Edge apps panel in One UI gives more space for your favorite programs if you need it.

The program drawer on a large Galaxy tablet might seem excessively vast and pointless. The home screen, taskbar, and optional Edge apps panel could all be used to keep all of your essential apps, while the ones you don't use could be hidden or added to a folder.

Why would you ever want the applications folder disabled?

One advantage of disabling the apps drawer on a Galaxy tablet is that the "Swipe up" home screen gesture is now usable for the "Search from Home Screen" feature. Users of the One UI can look up settings, applications, files, contacts, and more using this intelligent search engine. On tablets with big enough displays and room on the home screen, this intelligent search tool might be even more useful than the apps drawer.

How can the applications folder be replaced using "Search from Home Screen"?

If the thought of losing your customized home screen arrangement makes you nervous, don't be. If you use this technique and toggle Search for the applications drawer, you won't have to fear about ruining your current home screen. Your preferences will be kept.

You need to disable the applications drawer on your Galaxy tablet first things first. How to do it:

- Log into your tablet's settings.
- On the left side of the screen, choose "Home screen," then press "Home screen layout."
- Click "Apply" after selecting "Home screen only."

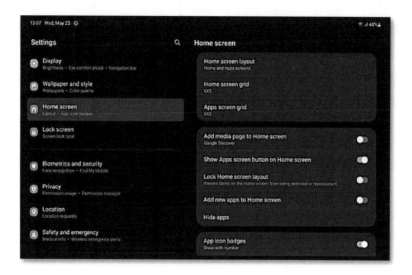

Keep in mind that the home screen settings for these two modes are distinct. You will discover all of your shortcuts and home screen settings just as you left them when you originally activated "Home screen only" should you choose to re-enable "Home and Apps screens."

The next and final step is to enable the "Search from Home Screen" feature after the applications drawer has been disabled.

How to do it:

- ❖ Activate settings and select "Home Screen"
- ❖ Scroll down and activate the "Search from Home" toggle located just to the right of the Home Screen menu.

I'm done! The smart search feature and your keyboard are now instantly accessible by swiping up from anywhere on the home screen.

WAYS OF NAVIGATION

Change the type of navigation panel

To navigate your phone, use the Navigation tab. The standard navigation buttons are positioned at the foot of the screen by default.

- Select Preferences > Display.
- Scroll down to the navigation bar.
- Select the type of menu you want.
- You can activate or disable the Navigation buttons' persistent display on the screen by selecting Full-Screen Gestures.

Step 4: Choose Additional options if you want to further personalize your navigation bar after choosing Full screen gestures.

Step 5: Set the sensitivity of your back motion and decide whether to swipe from the bottom or from the sides and bottom.

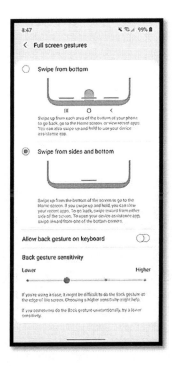

Menu navigational button order

The order of the icons on the Navigation bar is completely customizable.

- Select Preferences > Display.
- Scroll down and click the navigation box.
- Choose the desired setup under Button order. The changes are immediately effective.

Surprisingly, your decision will also affect where you move when using Swipe gestures.

The following are the three keys' functions:

1 Recents – Select this option to see a list of recently used applications.

2 Home - Tap to return to the Home Page. When you tap and keep, Google Assistant will launch.

3 Back: Tap here to return to the prior page.

PERSONALIZING HOME SCREENS

There should be a home page app.

Swipe up from the middle of the home screen to open the Applications tray. Pick the right app, move it to the top of the screen, and then place it where you want it on the home screen.

Note: It should be noted that you can also open the Apps tray by swiping up from the bottom of the home screen, selecting and holding the chosen app, and then choosing Add to Home. To add a widget (a tiny program) to the home screen, select and hold an empty area of the screen, then select Widgets.

- You can add or remove folders from the home screen.
- Drag the chosen app over a different app, then let go. It will automatically make a new folder.
- Select and hold the appropriate folder, then click Delete to remove it.
- To delete a folder, you can also choose and drag each app out of the folder.

Displays Available

To choose the preferred display choice, choose and hold an empty spot on the home screen, then follow these steps:

- **SET HOME SCREEN PANEL TO DEFAULT:** Choose the Home icon at the top of the screen after sliding to the preferred home screen panel.

• **TO ADD A WIDGET:** Choose Widgets, then pick the widget you want and drag it to the desired spot.

HOW TO CHANGE THE WALLPAPER: First, choose Wallpaper & Style, then find and choose the preferred wallpaper.

• **CHANGE SCREEN GRID:** Go to Settings > Home screen grid, choose the arrangement you want, and then click Save.

Tips

Home screen panels can be be added, moved, or eliminated as needed. A panel can be added by dragging an app onto an empty home screen, removed by removing all apps from a home screen, or moved by selecting the panel you want to move and dragging it there.

NOTIFICATION PANEL

Access notifications quickly and reply to them.

- From the Notifications bar, swipe downward. There will be notifications displayed.

- Choose the drop-down icon and the preferred reaction or action to respond to a notification.

Setup notification preferences.

1. From the notification bar, swipe down and choose the settings icon.

Then, choose Notifications. As desired, modify the notification settings.

Activate or deactivate notification badges

To turn notification badges on or off, go to the Notifications screen, select Advanced options, and then click the App icon badges switch.

Activate or deactivate lock screen notifications

Choose Notifications > Lock screen notifications > pick the Lock screen notifications switch from the Settings screen to enable or disable notifications from appearing when the device is locked.

Toggle notifications on or off for each individual app.

1. Scroll to and choose Apps from the Settings screen, then pick the required app.

2. Click Notifications. The Notification settings can then be modified as needed by selecting the Allow notifications switch.

Refine the notification sounds

- Choose Sounds and vibration from the Settings panel.

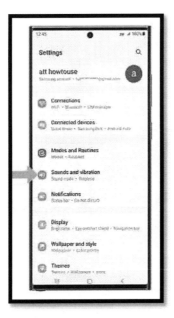

- Click on Sound of notification. Choose the notification sound you like, then click the back arrow.

EDGE PANEL AND ITS USAGE

Your favorite programs, functions, and contacts are easily accessible via Edge panels.

Activating the Edge Panel

Follow these steps to deploy the Edge Panels:

1. Access Settings

- On the Settings window, choose Display.

Note: For earlier devices, select Edge Screen from the Settings menu.

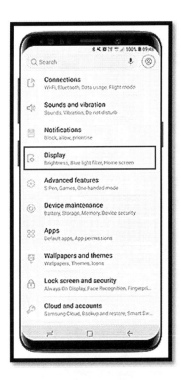

- Choose Edge Screen from the display screen menu.

- Edge Panels can be activated by left-to-right swiping the switch.

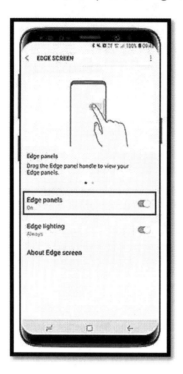

- The Edge Panel is now visible on the display.
- To access Edge Panels, swipe left.

- To pick the edge panels, swipe left or right.
- To change or see more Edge Panels, tap the Settings icon.

- To select your desired panels, swipe left or right.
- Please take note that you may only select nine panels at once.

Making changes to the edge panel handle

Position, height, and transparency of the handle can all be changed.

Do the following:

1. Center the screen by moving the Edge panel button there. If the Edge Panel is not visible, follow the directions under "How to enable Edge Panel" above.

2. Choose Preferences.

3. From the Additional options selection (three vertical dots) at the top of the screen, select Edge panel handle.

Note: To access options for the Edge panel handle on previous devices, swipe up from the bottom of the screen.

- Choose the option you wish to change by tapping it.

CHAPTER FIVE

CONTENT TRANSFER WITH SAMSUNG SMART SWITCH

Part 1

Wirelessly Transfer Data from an Android or iPhone to a Samsung S23 Ultra

You can keep your smartphone plugged into its charger while the transfer is happening thanks to the speed of wireless data transmission.

The procedures for transferring files from your old phone to your new Galaxy phone using Smart Switch are outlined below.

First, confirm that the Smart Switch software is loaded on both new and old phones. Maintain a tight proximity between the two phones as well.

- Open the Settings program on your new Galaxy phone and choose Accounts and backup.
- Next, choose Bring data from previous device.
- Select Receive data on your phone. Tap Send data on your previous phone.
- Check your previous phone's OS and select the appropriate source.
- Make a Wi-Fi selection. Launch Smart Switch on your old phone, connect, and then select Allow to accept all incoming connections.
- In the lower right corner, click Transfer after selecting the data you wish to migrate.
- Press Go to the Home screen after the transfer is finished.

Part 2:

Use A USB Cable To Transfer Info from An Android/iPhone Device To A Samsung S23 Ultra

Use a USB cord to connect your old phone and new phone so that files can be transferred rapidly.

The steps for using Smart Switch to transfer data to a Samsung S23 Ultra from an Android or iPhone are outlined below.

Step 1: Use a USB cable to connect your old and new phones. A USB connection might be necessary, depending on the previous phone.

Step 2: Click Smart Switch, followed by Receive data, after seeing the pop-up box for selecting an app.

Step 3: On the old phone, tap Accept. If you don't already have it, download the Smart Switch software from the Google Play Store or the Galaxy Store.

You'll be presented with a list of the data you can transfer as soon as your new phone detects the old one.

Step 4: Click Transfer after selecting the items you want to bring. Keep the USB cable connected to the phone while the transmission is happening.

IMPORT iCloud Contents

Security and privacy are of the utmost significance to Samsung. Samsung DOES NOT STORE YOUR APPLE ACCOUNT INFORMATION ON THE PHONE OR ELSEWHERE. Your Apple ID and password are only ever used to immediately log in to the iCloud backup service; they are never stored on the device or anywhere else. Through Smart Switch, you can transfer material to a Samsung device. It cannot transfer data to an iOS smartphone.

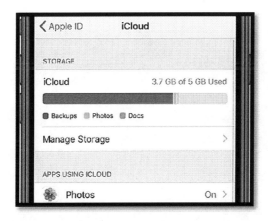

You must first sync your iOS phone with iCloud to ensure that all of your most recent stuff is prepared for transfer.

Go to Settings on your iOS device, then tap your Apple ID. Hit iCloud, then press the switches to choose which files to sync. Automatic synchronization will take place.

Note: Go to the iCloud setup site if you are unfamiliar with using iCloud.

Using a USB connection, move content.
- In order to transfer files between your new Galaxy phone and your iOS phone, you can also utilize a USB cable.
- Nevertheless, you will also require a MicroUSB to USB adapter in addition to the iOS cord that was packaged with your iOS phone (OTG cable).
- Furthermore, check that both phones are charged because you cannot charge them while the transfer is in progress.

- On the brand-new Galaxy phone, open Smart Switch, then hit Receive data.
- Tap iPad or iPhone. With a USB-OTG converter and the lightning wire from an iOS phone, join the two devices.
- You must tap Trust when adding a new trusted device, and you might then need to enter your phone's unlock code to confirm the trust.
- On the Galaxy phone, press Next.

- Tap Transfer after choosing the content you want to move.
- When done, on the new phone, touch Done, and on the old phone, tap Close.
- The Smart Switch software on a Galaxy phone offers alternatives for the Galaxy and iPhone.

A USB cable can be used to transfer the following information:

Contacts, a schedule, a calendar, messages, notes, call history, and bookmarks are examples of personal content.

Note: Smart Switch protects your private material. A Samsung device or a device from a third party will never have access to the encrypted data that is sent from the iCloud backup servers to your phone.

- App data includes Voice Memos, Documents, Photographs, Music (DRM-free content only), Videos, and Suggested Apps.
- Wi-Fi and alarms are among the settings.

Create a backup on a computer

You should also think about saving the data from your old phone to a Computer or Mac as a backup. In this manner, your data will still be available even if iCloud is unavailable or if you forget your Apple ID.

- Use a USB cable to connect your old phone to your computer, then tap Allow.

- Choose Backup after opening Smart Switch in your computer's browser.
- Choose the file formats you want to transfer, then click OK. Your data backup will start on your machine.
- A notification will show when it's finished to let you know; click OK.
- Computer's default location for saving data
- The files are kept in a default place when backing up data on a PC or Mac.
- If you like, you may also select a specific location.

The default locations are listed below to aid you in finding your stored data:

- C: Users [username] AppData Roaming Samsung Smart Switch PC Windows 8 Windows 7 Windows Vista
- C: Users [username] Documents in Windows 10
- Samsung\SmartSwitch
- Mac OS X: backup.Samsung/SmartSwitch/Users/[username]
- Choose Start to swiftly navigate to the AppData folder.
- Type "appdata" into the search box, and then press the Enter key.

Data synchronization using a computer

The data on your phone can also be synced with your PC or Mac. This guarantees that the material on your computer and phone will be identical.

On a PC

> ➢ Open Smart Switch on your PC, then choose Outlook Sync.
> ➢ Log in if necessary, using your Microsoft Outlook login information.
> ➢ Choose Outlook Sync Preferences after that.
> ➢ Choose what you wish to sync, after which click OK.
> ➢ When you're ready, choose Confirm after selecting Sync Now.
> ➢ Outlook Sync is highlighted in the PC or Mac version of the Smart Switch software.

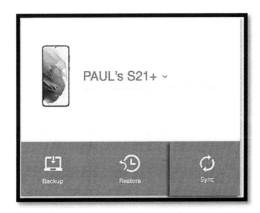

> ➢ Choose Sync Now after selecting the computer content you want to sync.
> ➢ Open Smart Switch on your Mac, then click Sync.
> ➢ Choose Confirm once the synchronizing is complete.

USE OF MICROSD CARD OR USB FLASH DRIVE

For the Samsung Galaxy S23 Ultra, what storage capacity is required?

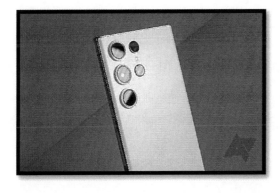

What choices are there for storage on the Device?

On the other hand, the Galaxy S23 Ultra came with a minimum of 256GB of internal storage. While the top-of-the-line S23 Ultra is available in 256GB, 512GB, and a 1TB model.

For data storage and restoration, use Samsung Cloud.

Not all regions may be enabled by Samsung Cloud, and Verizon phones may not support it either.

With Samsung Cloud, you can choose between manual and automated data backup. If you use the Automatic backup function, your data will be automatically backed up once every 24 hours while your Galaxy S23 ultra device is charging and connected to Wi-Fi. Additionally, you must switch off the screen for at least an hour.

Manual Reverse Open Preferences, after which pick your Samsung account name from the menu at the top of the screen. If you aren't already logged into your Samsung account, sign in by following the on-screen directions.

Choose the data you want to backup by selecting the switch after tapping Samsung Cloud (es). At the bottom of the screen, select Back up data, and then select Back up immediately.

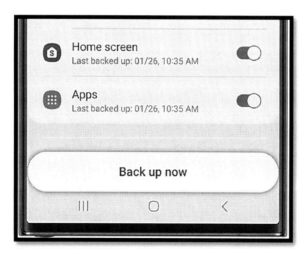

> The cloud backup will start to upload. If you have a lot of files, it can take some time.

Note: While the backup is running, you can switch to another screen. When it is finished, a notification will show up while it is still running in the background.

➢ After it's finished, tap Done.
➢ Tap More options (the three vertical dots), then touch Further details to find out more about the synchronizing procedure.

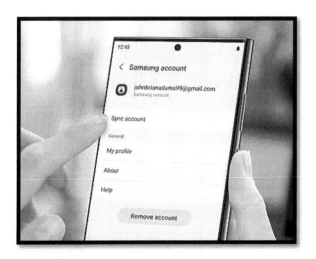

AUTOMATIC REVERSAL

➢ Open Settings, then select Accounts and backup from the menu.
➢ Choose your Samsung account by tapping Manage accounts.
➢ Choose Sync account.

Please take note, that if the Auto back up option is missing, this feature is not supported by your carrier. In the event that the cloud storage is full, content will not back up automatically.

On a Galaxy phone, the backup is automatic.

Backup Your Data

➢ Restoring your data is easy once everything has been backed up on Samsung Cloud.
➢ Open Settings, then select your Samsung account name from the list of options at the top of the screen.
➢ After selecting Samsung Cloud, choose Restore data.

➤ Choose the device backup you want, and then choose the content you wish to restore.

➤ If prompted, tap Install after tapping Restore.

➤ The download of the backup will start. If you have numerous files, it can take a while.

➤ Once it's done, tap Done.

Share with your Computer url for Windows

You may sync documents, photographs, and more between your Galaxy S23 ultra mobile and a PC by using Connect to Windows. Just make sure you've configured Phone Link and Link to Windows before beginning.

Choose Pictures in the Phone Connection app by finding it on your laptop and opening it. If they aren't there, click the Refresh symbol at the top, just below your S23's ultra-name, and wait a few seconds.

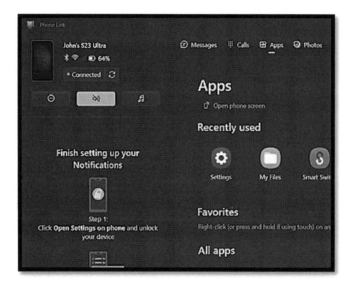

➤ After choosing a photo, make a selection from the options up above. To view and edit the photo, choose Open.

➤ You can send something to another device by sharing it, copying it, or saving it as to your computer. If necessary, choose Delete to remove the image.

➤ A picture can also be dragged and dropped onto your PC's desktop or into a folder.

> The Phone Connection app will erase outdated photo previews from your PC when you capture more photos on your S23. On the phone itself, no photos are ever modified or removed.

> To access these features from your Desktop, choose Messages, Calls, and Apps.

HOW TO COPY DATA FROM WINDOWS PHONE

❖ Transfer Media Files to/from PC on the Galaxy S23 Ultra

❖ This facilitates the movement of images, videos, and music between your device and a computer.

❖ These techniques can only transfer video and music that are DRM-free or unprotected.

❖ To transfer files on a Macintosh® computer, additional software is needed.

❖ Check out this video for a brief introduction to Verizon Cloud, which may be used to store media.

❖ Upload images or videos to a computer

❖ Use the included USB cord to connect the gadget to a computer.

❖ Tap Accept when asked to give access to your data.

❖ Touch and hold the Status bar (at the top) if necessary, then slide it to the bottom.

❖ Tap for other USB alternatives can be found in the "Android System" section.

❖ Decide on Moving files.

❖ When a blue dot is seen, it is selected.

❖ Launch "Windows Explorer" or "File Explorer."

❖ Press the Windows+E (Windows key logo+E) keys on the keyboard.

❖ Instead, select "Open Windows Explorer" or "File Explorer" from the context menu when you right-click Start.

❖ Navigate using "File" or "Windows Explorer": Galaxy S23Phone.

❖ This PC's list includes the Galaxy S23 5G.

Launch "Windows Explorer" or "File Explorer."

❖ Press the Windows+E (Windows key logo+E) keys on the keyboard.

❖ Instead, select "Open Windows Explorer" or "File Explorer" from the context menu when you right-click Start.

❖ Navigate using "File" or "Windows Explorer": Phone Galaxy S23.

❖ The Galaxy S23 may be found in the "This Computer" section.

Device names that suit the model of your device include Galaxy S23+ and Galaxy S23 Ultra.

The following folders on the computer to copy video or image files into the relevant folder(s) on the phone:

Movies & Pictures

❖ The USB cord should be unplugged from the PC.

Music File Transfer to PC

❖ Use the included USB cord to connect the gadget to a computer.

❖ Tap Accept when asked to give access to your data.

❖ Touch and hold the Status bar (at the top) if necessary, then slide it to the bottom.

❖ Tap for other USB alternatives can be found in the "Android System" section.

❖ Decide on Moving files.

❖ When a blue dot is seen, it is selected.

❖ Launch "Windows Explorer" or "File Explorer."

❖ Press the Windows+E (Windows key logo+E) keys on the keyboard.

❖ Instead, select "Open Windows Explorer" or "File Explorer" from the context menu when you right-click Start.

❖ Navigate using "File" or "Windows Explorer": Phone Galaxy S23 ultra.

❖ The Galaxy S23 ultra may be found in the "This Computer" section.

CHAPTER SIX

PHONE CALLS

Set Wi-Fi Calling on or Off on a Samsung Galaxy S23

To enable or disable Wi-Fi Calling on your Galaxy S23 Ultra, adhere to these thorough steps.

When turned on, Wi-Fi Calling might improve the caliber of conversations made inside.

- To use Wi-Fi Calling, make sure your Wi-Fi is turned on and linked.
- Wi-Fi conversations always begin in the US, even if you are outside of it.
- Calls to US lines are free of charge (except for 411 or other premium calls).
- The cost of calls to foreign numbers will depend on your international long-distance plan.
- To call, tap the Phone symbol on a home screen (lower-left).
- If unavailable, slide up from the middle of the display and choose Phone.
- To navigate, click the Settings menu button.
- Tap the button to turn on Switch on or off Switch off Wi-Fi Calling.

If you're first setting up Wi-Fi Calling:

• To proceed after perusing the Terms & Conditions, tap CONTINUE.

• Ensure that the checkbox next to Terms & Conditions is chosen.

• After inputting the E911 address for the emergency spot, press SAVE.

This information is sent to the emergency dispatcher during every 911 Wi-Fi contact. In the event that address validation is unsuccessful, you must enter a legitimate address once more.

After the address has been properly validated, Wi-Fi Calling becomes operational.

Make sure Wi-Fi calling is enabled, touch Roaming network preference, choose "Wi-Fi preferred" or "Cellular preferred," then restart the device to choose your calling preference while traveling outside the Verizon wireless coverage area or abroad.

MAKE A PHONE CALL

The Phone icon will appear in the Notification bar while you are on an active call.

Call-in options

The following choices will be available when on an active call:

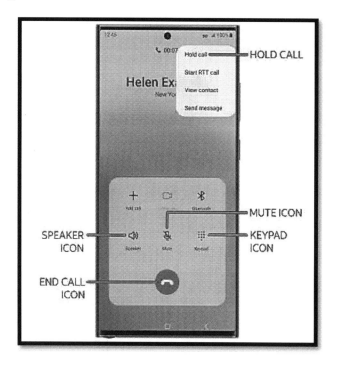

• **HOLD/RESUME CALL:** Choose Hold call by clicking the menu icon.

• **KEYPAD SHOW/HIDE:** Click the Keypad symbol.

• **TO USE/DISUSE A PHONE AS A SPEAKER,** Choose THE SPEAKER ICON.

MUTE/UNMUTE: Click on the mute icon.

• **END CALL:** Click the icon labeled "End call."

Employ Speed Dial

- Choose and hold the desired Speed dial number on the keyboard.
- A number can be added to your speed dial by choosing the dots menu icon, choosing Speed dial numbers, and then entering the appropriate contact.

- While on a call, use your phone.
- Selecting the Home key will bring up the home screen while you are on a call.
- Sliding down from the notification bar and choosing Active call will take you back to an active call.

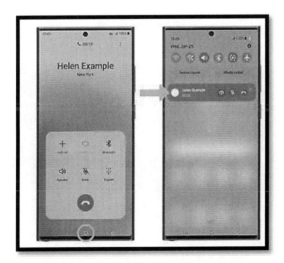

SET UP a conference call.

Choose the Add call icon from an active call, then follow the on-screen instructions. Choose the End call icon to end a call.

You must choose Merge to merge the two calls when setting up a conference call after connecting with a second caller. In both individual and conference calls, the End call icon is the same.

Reject a call by text message instead

- Swipe up from the bottom of the screen to reject a call and send a text message when you receive one.
- Choose the text message you want to send, or choose Create a new message to compose your own.

Note: From the home screen, choose the phone app > menu menu icon > Settings > Quick refuse texts > the desired message to change to write or amend text message replies.

ANSWERING CALLS

Want to answer calls quickly without scrolling the screen? In your Accessibility settings, merely turn on the Assistant menu. Please refer to the step-by-step instructions below.

1.Go to Settings and select Accessibility.

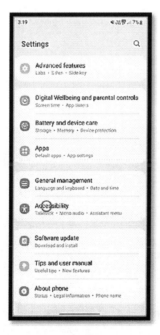

2 Pick dexterity and interaction

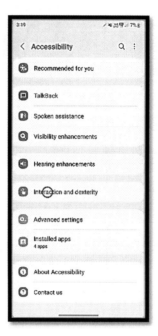

3 Select the Assistant menu.

4 Turn this option on.

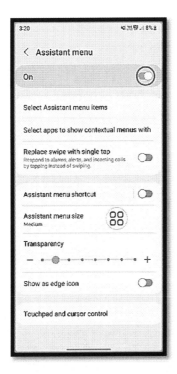

5 Turn on Swap Swipe for Single Touch.

You will be able to reply to alarms and alerts by tapping rather than swiping once this setting is activated.

6 From this point forward, you may just tap the icon for the call to answer or decline it when it comes in.

Blocking Hidden Or Unknown Numbers

Unknown/hidden phone numbers as well as new phone numbers can be blocked.

Step 1: Launch the Phone app, then select Settings from the More options menu (three vertical dots).

Step 2: Choose Block numbers > Turn on Block Unknown or Hidden Numbers.

Step 3: If you want to ban a certain phone number, add it.

RINGTONES AND CALL NOTIFICATIONS

Call notifications, ringtones, vibration patterns, and keypad tones can all be customized.

Step 1: Launch the Phone app, then select Settings from the More options menu (three vertical dots).

Step 2: Click Ringtones and call notifications.

Step 3: Change the keypad tones, ringtones, and call alerts.

Setting For Taking And Terminating Calls

1. Launch the Phone app, then select Settings from the More options menu (three vertical dots).

2. Tap Accepting and terminating calls.

3. Modify the choices for responding and terminating calls.

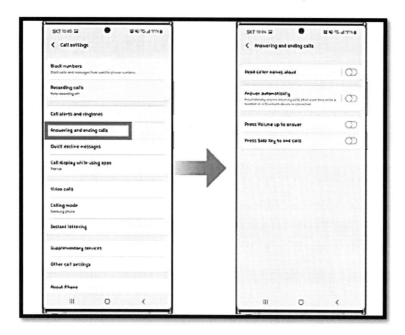

SETTING FOR QUICK DECLINE MESSAGES

Sending a message while ignoring an incoming call is possible.

Step 1: Launch the Phone app, then select Settings from the More options menu (three vertical dots).

Step 2: Choose Messages for quick decline.

Step 3: Modify messaging for Quick Decline.

VIDEO CALLS

When talking on the phone isn't enough to keep in touch with friends or family when you're apart, you can use video calls on your Galaxy phone, tablet, or computer to see them in person. There are already a lot of services available, along with some other choices and apps. Even if you won't be spending time with your loved ones in person, being able to view them in real time is the next best thing.

Please take note that not all carriers or devices may support this feature. Only when Android OS is used on both devices is video calling possible.

Built-in video calling and chat

You might be able to initiate a video call while you are already on the phone, depending on your carrier. Simply press the Video call icon to start a call when using the Phone app. It may be found between the Bluetooth and Add call icons. Tap the Camera icon to turn off your device's camera and return to a regular voice call. Depending on your carrier, this might change. You might need to end the call and dial back if you can't use the icon to return to a voice call.

- A Galaxy phone's call screen in the Phone app has a video call option.
- On some One UI 2 devices, the dialer includes Google Duo.
- The Google Duo icon might be replaced on some devices by the Video call icon.
- Google Duo, WhatsApp, and other video call options

The video chat app Google Duo is even preinstalled on the majority of Samsung handsets! Be sure to look in the Google folder on the Applications screen if you haven't already if it's not there on your device. It's simple to set up. Simply log into your Google account and complete a few simple steps.

The Google Duo icon may be seen in the Phone app for Samsung phones with One UI 2 depending on their provider.

Some additional third-party applications, like WhatsApp, Facebook, Skype, and Snapchat, also provide video chat. You have a wide range of choices when it comes to placing video calls; these are just a few of them. Utilize one of these apps or a program that you are accustomed to. On the Galaxy Store and Play Store, there are a ton of more alternatives.

Video call on your PC

You may also use your Galaxy Book or another Samsung Computer to video chat if you prefer to view your loved ones on a big screen. Two well-liked platforms for group video chats are Google Duo and Skype. You can even call relatives who live in other countries using Skype's translate feature.

Google Hangouts, WhatsApp, Zoom, Webex, and Discord are a few additional video chat applications.

Using a Samsung device, a woman and a man are video chatting.

For some functionality, some apps may require a premium subscription.

VIEW AND DELETE CALL HISTORY

Call logs maintain track of your phone usage and activities by recording all incoming, outgoing, missed, and rejected calls.

How to access call records

Step 1: Open the phone application icon.

Step 2: Choose Recents. The list of recent calls is available here.

Visit the Phone app if you want to see calls that fall under a particular category.

Step 1: Touch Recents, then hit the top-right filter options icon.

Step 2: Choose an option from the list:

- All calls
- Missed calls
- Rejected calls
- Outgoing calls
- Incoming calls

THE SAMSUNG S23 ULTRA AND VOICEMAIL

Before you can utilize Visual Voicemail, you must first set up voicemail. You can also access your voicemail by picking the Phone app from the home screen, pressing and holding the 1 key, entering your voicemail password if necessary, and then listening to your messages by following the on-screen prompts. Once your voicemail password has been reset, you won't be able to access voicemail if you've forgotten your current password.

- The Voicemail icon Voicemail icon will show up in the Notification bar when a new voicemail is received.
- Access a voicemail and listen to it.
- The phone app can be chosen from the home screen.

ACCESS: Click the Visual Voicemail button under the Keypad tab.

LISTEN: Choose your preferred voicemail.

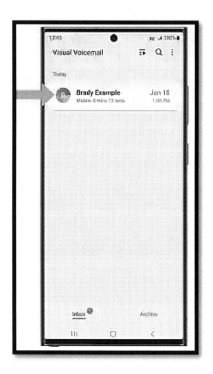

Consult the voicemail menu

- Choose the relevant icon.

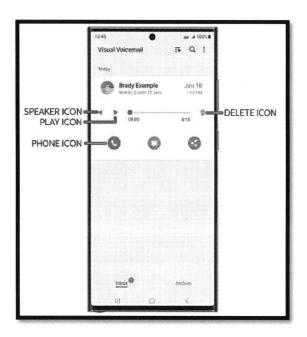

94

- **PLAY/PAUSE:** To play the message, click the Play icon. To stop the message, click the Pause icon.

- **SPEAKER:** To enable or disable speaker mode, select the Speaker icon.

- **CALL BACK:** To call the phone number again, select the Phone symbol.

- **DELETE:** To remove a voicemail, click the Delete symbol.

MORE OPTIONS: Choose the preferred voicemail, hold it in place, and then choose the preferred choice.

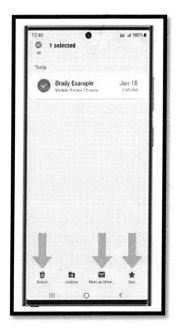

- **DELETE:** To remove the voicemail, choose Delete. To confirm, select Delete once more.

MARK AS UNHEARD: Choose Mark as Unheard, and then choose OK to confirm.

- **STAR:** To mark a voicemail as favorite, select Star, and then OK to confirm.

For advice on how to manage your voicemail, see Access voicemail messages. For solutions to typical voicemail issues, visit Troubleshoot Voicemail.

95

CHAPTER SEVEN

APPLICATION CONTACTS for S23 ULTRA

Swipe up from the screen's center to reveal the Apps tray, where you may then choose the Contacts app to access your contacts.

Create a contact

1. Click the Add icon, then choose the Contact save location of your choice.

2. Fill in the relevant areas with the necessary contact details. To modify the account to which you want to store the contact, select the drop-down icon. Choose the Picture icon and then go to the chosen image to add. After you're done, click Save.

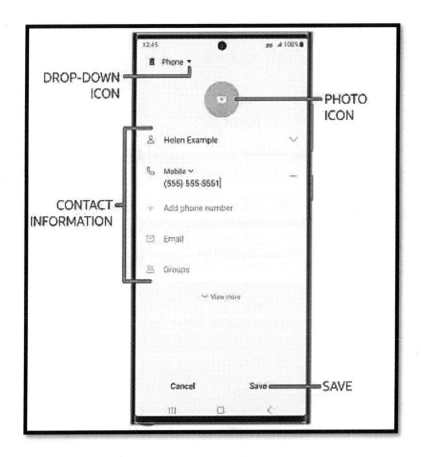

DROP-DOWN ICON

PHOTO ICON

CONTACT INFORMATION

SAVE

CHANGE OR ELIMINATE A CONTACT

EDIT CONTACT: After choosing the desired contact, click the Edit icon. If necessary, edit the contact, then choose Save.

REMOVE CONTACT: Click the menu icon, then choose Delete. Choosing Move will confirm.

INSERT A RINGTONE

Choose See more from the edit contact screen, then scroll to and choose Ringtone. Use the Back arrow after choosing the desired Ringtone.

MAKE A CONTACT BACKUP

- Choose Manage Contacts from the Contacts screen, then Import or Export Contacts, then follow the on-screen directions.

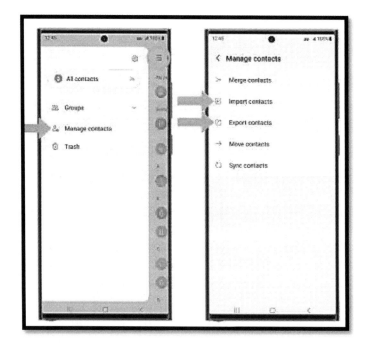

EDITING CONTACTS

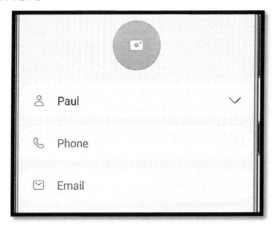

- Tap the contact you wish to edit after opening the Contacts app.
- Click Edit.
- By tapping the required field, you can edit the information for your contact.
- Tap on the field you'd like to add numbers or email addresses to, and then tap + Add.
- You can remove something by tapping the Delete (minus) icon next to it.
- To change more options like address, remarks, relationship, etc., tap See more.
- Tap Save once you're finished editing.

MANAGEMENT OF PHONE CONTACTS

99

Build Your Image

To access your contact information, you typically switch between several different applications, including your email.

Make a profile in the Contacts program and store all of your contact information there instead.

Launch Connections by going there. Select your name at the top of the page.

Reminder: You can also access your profile by tapping your name at the top of the screen after accessing Settings.

> ➢ Log in to your Samsung Account if necessary.
> ➢ All of your details, including your phone number, email, emergency contacts, and more, will be listed once you log in.
> ➢ To edit the information you want, click Edit at the bottom of the page.

> ➢ Tap Save in the bottom right corner when you're done.
> ➢ Now, it will be simple to locate your profile and contact details in an emergency situation, such as if you misplace your device.
> ➢ You also have the choice of using Google to backup and sync your contacts, Samsung Cloud to sync data between your other devices, and both.

Manage duplicate contacts

> ➤ Things can become complicated if your partner continues receiving new numbers.
> ➤ Just link them together so that their name doesn't appear more than once in your Contacts.
> ➤ Go to Contacts, then select Menu (the three horizontal lines).
> ➤ After selecting Manage contacts, select Merge contacts.
> ➤ Duplicate phone numbers, emails, or names can all be combined. Tap Merge after selecting the repeats.
> ➤ Choose your favorite contacts.
> ➤ You can make someone your favorite contact if you frequently phone or text them, such as your best buddy.
> ➤ Go to Contacts and select Add your favorite contacts from the list at the top.

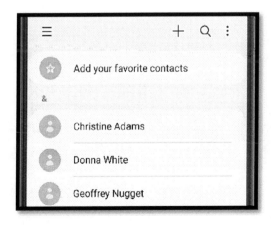

- To find someone, you may either swipe through the list or search for a contact's name. Choose the contact or contacts you want, and then press Done.
- The chosen contact or contacts will then show up under Favorites at the top. They will however continue to show up in the general contacts list down below.

Reminder: After choosing a contact, touch Favorites (the star icon) at the bottom to add more favorite contacts. Yellow will appear on the icon.

Also, your preferred contacts can be reordered. Use the arrows to drag and drop your contacts into the desired position after selecting Reorder Favorites from the More options menu on the Contacts screen. To reorder your favorite contacts, you must have at least two of them.

Simply choose the desired contact, then press Favorites, to remove them from your favorites. White will appear on the icon.

Create a Group

You have a lot of work to do, therefore everything, even your contacts, must be entirely professional. No worries, you can segregate your personal and professional lives by creating a Group under Contacts that will only allow you to see specific connections.

- Go to Contacts, hit Menu (the three horizontal lines), and then tap Groups to get the contact list.

- After selecting New Group, give the group a name. Moreover, you can alter a group ringtone.
- Choose the contacts you want to add to the group by tapping Add member, and then touch Done.
- Click Save.

At any time, you can add current or new contacts to the group you just created.

Block a contact

If the need ever arises, you can ban and unblock contacts using the Phone and Contacts applications. Certain models have a Smart Call feature that can identify numbers that are not in your contact list and let you to ban them. You can avoid this if you frequently get voicemails from unknown callers.

Controlling Contact Storage

You can transfer your contact information to a SIM card if you need to keep it somewhere else. Just make sure your gadget has a SIM card in it before you start.

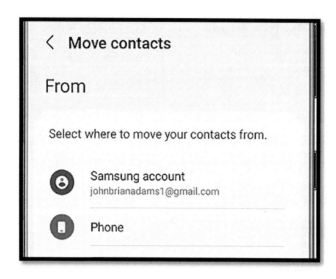

Open the Contacts app by going to its location.

Move contacts after selecting Manage contacts from the menu (the three horizontal lines).

Choose your preferred option, then hit Done after choosing your desired contact or contacts.

Tap Move after choosing the new location to send the contact(s) to.

CHAPTER EIGHT

MESSAGES

SENDING AN SOS MESSAGES IN S23 ULTRA

If you're in a situation where you don't feel comfortable and need to issue an emergency alert, you can call for assistance using the SOS messaging function on Galaxy smartphones and smart watches.

You can automatically call and message up to four pre-designated contacts using the SOS messaging feature without having to dial their numbers.

After configured, pressing your lock button three times will generate an alert. This immediately notifies your chosen contacts of your location and sends them an SOS message with a Google map link. Also, a five-second audio recording and images from your smartphone's front and back cameras are shared with others using this service.

1 Start your Settings > Advanced Settings menu.

2. Click Send SOS message after scrolling down the page.

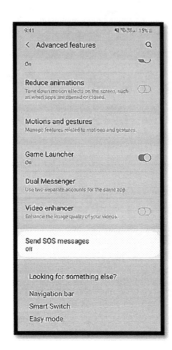

3 Turn on the SOS button and select OK from the pop-up message.

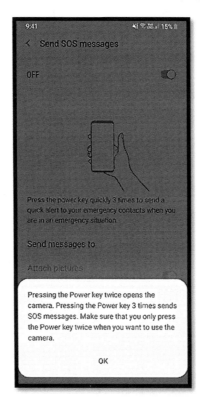

4.After reading the terms and conditions, click the Agree button to move on to the following stage.

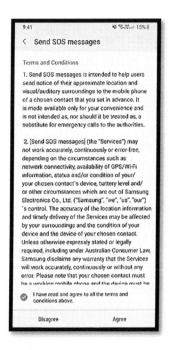

5 Press Add to add a contact for emergencies.

6.After creating an emergency contact, tap Add. When finished, tap the back arrow button to save your changes.

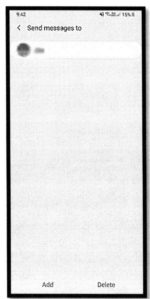

7.On/Off switch Embedding images or audio recordings

Tap Send messages to, enter your selected emergency contact information, and then tap Add more emergency contacts if you decide to do so later.

8.Press the power button three times quickly to swiftly send SOS texts to your emergency contacts. Depending on the SOS message choices you have selected, the text may also contain images and audio messages.

You may see the SOS Message's status by swiping down to open your notification panel.

9.The receiving emergency contact will be sent a link directly to Google Maps when the SOS message has been received, allowing them to find your precise location. Also, they will be able to examine any MMS-sent images and audio files.

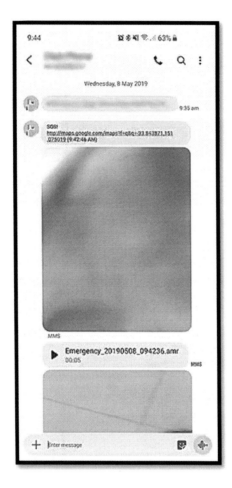

HOW TO READ MESSAGES I RECEIVED

Looking at a message

You'll get a notification in your messaging app when you get a message; to view it, do the following:

1.Choose Messages from the Samsung folder on the home screen or slide up to reach your apps and select Messages.

2. A list of your conversations will appear when you first launch the app. The list's top section will show new messages, and any unread ones will have a blue number next to them (the number indicates the number of unread messages in a conversation).

3. Open and read a message by tapping it.

4.After reading the message, you have the option of responding by entering in the chat message box.

5. To send your message, touch the send icon after you've completed writing it.

A message being sent

In order to create and send a text message, you must:

1.Messages may be accessed from the Samsung folder by swiping up from the home screen or by selecting it directly from the list of apps.

2 Click the Compose button.

3.The contact you want to message can be chosen by tapping the addition (+) sign.

You can directly enter the recipient's phone number in the Recipient box if you wish to send a message to someone who is not a contact.

4 Press Done.

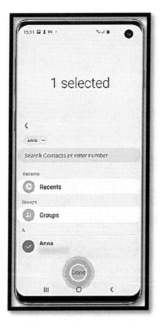

5 After finishing your message, tap the Send button.

Please be aware that if you exit a message before sending it, it will be preserved as a draft.

Sending an MMS

Please be aware that your network operator may charge you for MMS or multimedia messages or may even forbid them based on your contract. If you have issues sending or getting MMS, check with your network to see if they are covered by your contract.

An MMS, or Multimedia Message, is a text communication that includes media attachments.

You must: in order to send an MMS.

1.Select Messages from the Samsung folder on the home screen or slide up to reach your apps and select Messages.

2 Click the Compose button.

3. The contact you want to message can be chosen by tapping the addition (+) sign.

4 Press Done.

5 By clicking the Picture icon, you can upload a photo from your gallery, snap a new photo with the Camera icon, or attach an existing photo.

6 Choose a multimedia component and tap it.

7 Press Send. Your smartphone may require that you hit Done before moving on.

Please get in touch with your network operator if you are having trouble sending an MMS.

Indicate when text messages have been read and delivered.

You can enable settings to have a notification appear when your message has been read or delivered. To activate this:

1 Launch the messaging app.

2 Press menu (three dots).

3 Choose Setting.

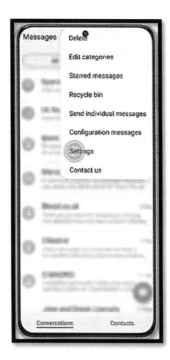

4 Choose More options.

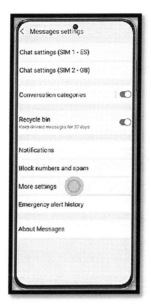

5 Choose whether you want to turn on text messages or multimedia messages by tapping one of those options.

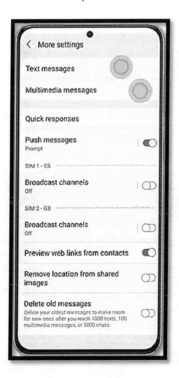

6 Slide the switch to enable Display when read or Delivered.

7 The word "Delivered" will appear next to a text message once it has been sent.

8 "Read" will appear next to a text message once it has been read.

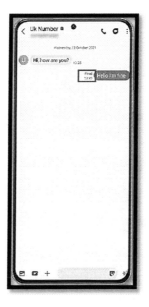

Deletion of a message

You must: to remove an SMS message;

1.Messages may be accessed from the Samsung folder by swiping up from the home screen or by selecting it directly from the list of apps.

2 Either hold down the message(s) you want to remove or hit All.

3. Press Delete.

4 Hit Delete once more.

5.The message(s) you sent have been deleted.

Message forwarding

You can use the device's built-in forwarding feature by following the procedures listed below.

1.Messages may be accessed from the Samsung folder by swiping up from the home screen or by selecting it directly from the list of apps.

2 Start by opening the message you want to forward.

3.The message content will pop up with a menu if you press and hold it.

4 Touch the forward arrow.

5 After choosing your contact or contacts, tap Write or Done. Go to step 6 if you don't see this screen.

6.Select Send.

Message blocking

In order to ban text messages, you must:

1.Messages may be accessed from the Samsung folder by swiping up from the home screen or by selecting it directly from the list of apps.

2 Go to the blocked message and open it.

3 select the menu (three dots).

4 Choose "Block number" or "Block contact."

Tap Unblock number or Unblock contact to take the phone number off your list of blocked numbers.

5.Select Block.

You must: in order to scan your spam folder for text messages;

1 On the home screen, select Messages, or slide up to access your apps and select Messages from the Samsung folder.

2 Press menu (three dots).

3.Click Settings.

4.To stop receiving texts, select Block numbers and messages.

5 Click on Blocked messages.

6.There will now be a display of any blocked communications.

Using My Emoji to Send a Message

When using the built-in emojis or smilies, a normal-length SMS shouldn't cost anything (160 characters). If you use emojis from a third-party keyboard, your Text could become an MMS and result in charges from your network.

You can use My Emoji to communicate in funny and unique ways. Create an emoji that perfectly represents you!

You can share stickers to friends and family as well as take pictures and movies using My Emoji.

1.Messages may be accessed from the Samsung folder by swiping up from the home screen or by selecting it directly from the list of apps.

2 Choose the compose button.

3.Choose the Emoji symbol using the Samsung keyboard. Choose the smiley face to modify your keyboard settings if you can't see this option.

4 Choose the emoji that you want to utilize.

5.Select Send

Send a text by voice

You must: in order to send a text message by voice.

1.Messages may be opened from the Samsung folder by swiping up from the home screen or by selecting it directly from the list of apps.

2 Click the Compose button.

3 Touch the microphone icon after tapping to enter the message.

Certain operating systems will show a radio wave icon. You will be able to leave a voicemail using this, but it will be sent as an MMS, which could result in fees from your network provider.

4. Begin speaking. Now, the device should type whatever you say.

5. Press Send.

CHAPTER NINE

PHONE SETTINGS

DARK MODE

Your phone or tablet might as well be the sun in the evening, even though you might not observe it during the day. The brilliant screen can make you squint, so you might remain up until the early hours. Don't fear; your Samsung phone has the answer. It was referred to as Night mode or Black mode in earlier iterations. In order to use your phone or tablet more easily at night, you should have a darker theme installed. Additionally, you can use Eye comfort shield to lessen the blue light from the screen and extremely dim to completely obscure the screen.

Note: Using Dark mode or Night mode with specific apps may cause flickering. Keep the software on your smartphone and apps updated to avoid this problem.

Set the Night or Dark setting manually.

Note: Dark mode might not work correctly if you're using a third-party app, a downloaded theme, or a typeface with high contrast.

When you choose Dark mode, all of your device's menus, settings, and factory-installed Samsung applications will have a darker theme. Some apps from third parties won't alter, though.

Use two fingertips to slide down from the top of the screen to reveal the Quick settings panel.

Next, swipe to and select the Night or Dark mode icon. The icon will glow when the setting is on.

To leave the setting, click the icon once more.

NOTE: You can also access Dark mode from the top of the Display settings screen on smartphones running Android 10 or later.

Schedule the use of the Dark or Night modes.

Simply set it to automatically turn on or off at a specific time if you occasionally forget to enable Dark mode or Night mode.

To access the Quick settings panel, first use two fingers to slide down from the top of the screen. To access the settings page for the Dark mode or Night mode, touch and hold the corresponding icon.

Press the button next to turn on when it's time. If you want Dark mode to automatically turn on in the evening and turn off in the morning, select Sunset to sunrise.

To create your own timetable for Dark mode, select Custom schedule. After selecting your desired Start time, tap Set schedule. Tap End after that, choose an End time, and then tap Done.

Note: You can manually activate or deactivate Dark mode whenever you wish, even if you have planned time for it.

Turn on the eye comfort screen.

The new Eye comfort shield choice is available on One UI 3.1 devices. Turn this on to lessen the quantity of blue light coming from your screen. As opposed to the traditional Blue light filter, a special algorithm will change the hue of your screen depending on environmental factors like how bright the outside light is.

The Quick settings panel can be accessed by using two fingertips to swipe down from the top of the screen. Navigate to and select the Eye comfort shield symbol.

 You can add the Eye comfort shield icon if it does not already exist in your Quick settings panel. When activated, the symbol will glow blue and your screen's hue will first have a faint yellow tint before becoming more neutral.

The Eye Comfort Shield icon can be touched and held to change the settings. Choose Adaptive to have the colors on the screen change based on the time of day or Custom to set the timetable and color temperature that work best for you.

Here are your choices for Custom:

Set a timetable: Choose from Custom, Sunset to Sunrise, or Always on to keep Eye Comfort Shield active at all times. Using Custom, you may choose the precise moment when Eye Comfort Shield should turn on and off.

Change the screen's color temperature by sliding the slider.

ADJUST BRIGHTNESS SETTING
Galaxy S23 Ultra - Change Display Settings and Brightness

To change the display/font settings and brightness settings, follow these instructions:

Elevate the brightness settings
- To access the applications screen from a Home Screen, swipe up from the screen's middle.
- These guidelines only apply to Standard Mode and the Home Screen's default configuration.
- Click the Settings icon to navigate.

Display.

- To change the brightness, move the blue bar in the 'Brightness' section to the left or right.
- To activate the On Switch icon or deactivate the Off Switch icon, tap Adaptive brightness.
- This option maximizes brightness for the light source that is available.

CHANGE THE DISPLAY AND FONT OPTIONS
- ❖ To access the applications screen from a Home Screen, swipe up from the screen's middle.
- ❖ These guidelines only apply to Standard Mode and the Home Screen's default configuration.
- ❖ **Navigate:** Settings Show Settings icon.
- ❖ For font size and style, tap.

Tap Font style, then pick one of the options below:

Default

❖ Downloadable fonts for SamsungOne Gothic Bold
❖ Toggle the Bold font switch on or off by tapping it.
❖ Touch and hold the blue dot in the "Font size" box, then move it left or right to the appropriate selection.
❖ To get back to the display settings screen, tap the Back symbol in the upper-left corner of the screen.
❖ Choose how large or tiny you want items on your screen to appear by tapping Screen zoom.
❖ Touch and hold the blue dot, then drag it left or right to the relevant selection to choose a size.
❖ To get back to the display settings screen, tap the Back symbol.
❖ Choose an option by tapping Screen timeout (e.g., 15 seconds, 30 seconds, 1 minute, etc.).
❖ To get back to the display settings screen, tap the Back symbol.
❖ To manage the phone's charging or docking behavior:
❖ Choose Screen Saver.
❖ When on, choose a choice (e.g., Colors, Photo Table, etc.).
❖ When the blue circle (left) appears, it is chosen.

SCREEN TIMEOUT

With the help of a setting on Samsung devices dubbed Screen Timeout, the screen will be turned off to save battery life. 30 seconds are the predetermined default value. Follow these steps to change the Screen Timeout option so that your phone or tablet's screen remains on for longer. The maximum Screen Timeout time is 10 minutes, but if you want to leave the screen on for as long as you are looking at it, you may want to turn on the Smart Stay option.

1 Open your Settings and select Display.

2 Click "Screen timeout."

3 Choose the screen timeout you want.

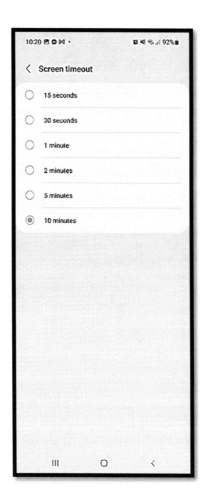

FONT SIZE AND STYLE

You can adjust the text size and style on your Galaxy phone if the font is too small to read. You can also download other typefaces to further personalize the display.

If you want to modify your font settings, see the guide below:

1.Change the font size and style.

 ❖ You can select a font size or design that suits you. Make the font look small, large, or bold. Follow the instructions below to alter your font's size or style.
 ❖ Then, open the Settings application, and then choose Display.

2.Choose the font size and style

3. At this point, you can change the options as needed.

- ❖ Drag the slider left or right to alter the font size.
- ❖ To make the typeface appear bolder, tap the toggle next to Bold font.
- ❖ To switch to a different font or download one, tap Font style.

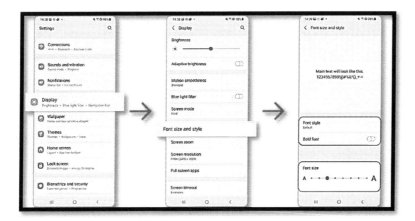

Install a new font

You may switch things up if you get tired of using the same old fonts by downloading a new font. Follow the directions below to obtain more fonts.

Then, open the Settings application, and then choose Display.

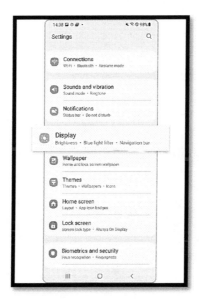

Make use of high contrast fonts.

If you like the font size and style you are presently using but wish you could read it more clearly, try turning on High contrast. As a result, every font will have an outline, making them stick out on the screen. To enable High contrast, follow the instructions below.

Start the Settings application, then choose Accessibility.

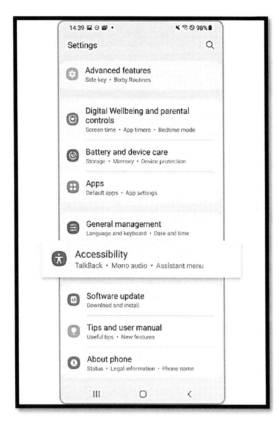

CHAPTER TEN

SOUND AND VIBRATION SETTING ON S23 ULTRA

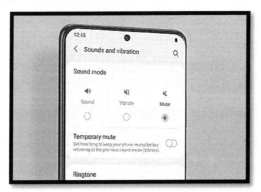

You can receive notification when you receive a text message, email, phone call, or system alert on your Galaxy phone or tablet in a number of different methods. These notification settings can be modified if you want your device to vibrate, play a sound, or notify you using a Bluetooth audio device. Your gadget also offers cutting-edge audio options like Dolby Atmos.

Customize noises, vibrations, and notifications

Control the sounds and vibrations that indicate notifications, screen taps, and other activities so that you always know what kind of alert you are getting.

You may also order the notifications you want to view first in the app alerts.

Change the music mode of your device without using the Volume keys. By swiping down from the top of the screen and tapping the Settings button, you can reach this by bringing up the Quick settings panel. By clicking Sounds and vibration, then, select a setting. You have the choice of Sound, Vibrate, or Silence.

Use the sound mode option rather than the Volume keys to change the sound mode without changing your customized sound levels.

Below is a summary of the sound settings for the Galaxy phone:

The frequency and power of your device's movements can be changed. By swiping down from the top of the screen and tapping the Settings button, you can reach this by bringing up the Quick settings panel. By selecting Sounds and vibration, select Vibrate. The options for Vibration strength, Call vibration pattern, and Notification vibration pattern can then be changed.

Media level, system sounds, notification volume, and call ringtone volume can all be changed. By swiping down from the top of the screen and tapping the Settings button, you can reach this by bringing up the Quick settings panel. Select Volume after choosing Noises and Vibration. Move the sliders for each sort of sound after that.

Note: The Volume keys can also be used to change the volume. Pressing it displays the volume level and current sound type in a pop-up menu. Toggle the sliders for the other sound kinds to change the volume after tapping the menu to expand it.

Ringtone: You can upload your own sounds or select from pre-made ones to personalize the call ringtone. You may access this by opening the Quick settings panel by swiping down from the top of the screen, then tapping the Settings button. Next select Ringtone from the Sounds and vibration menu. By opening the Contacts app, selecting a contact, and then selecting Modify, you may also give particular contacts ringtones. Then select Ringtone from the See More menu. To utilize an audio file as a ringtone, simply press Add (the plus sign) or a ringtone to hear a preview and pick it.

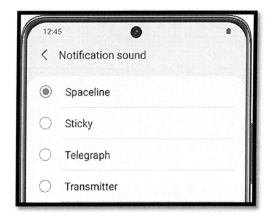

Choose a default notification alert sound for all notifications. You may access this by opening the Quick settings panel by swiping down from the top of the screen, then tapping the Settings button. After selecting Sounds and vibration, select Notification sound. To preview and choose a sound, tap on it.

Notification sounds for each app can also be customized using the App settings menu.

System sound: Choose a sound theme to be used for touch interactions, charging, switching between sound modes, Samsung Keyboard, and more. You may access this by opening the Quick settings panel by swiping down from the top of the screen, then tapping the Settings button. After selecting Sounds and vibration, select System sound. Pick a sound from the options.

Choose which applications provide notifications and how notifications notify you to prioritize and streamline app alerts. You may access this by opening the Quick settings panel by swiping down from the top of the screen, then tapping the Settings button. To choose a pop-up style, tap Notifications. You can personalize the notifications by selecting between Short and Detailed options.

Check out a list of the apps that have recently issued notifications. You may access this by opening the Quick settings panel by swiping down from the top of the screen, then tapping the Settings button. Tap Notifications, then select the one you want under Recently sent. To extend the list, press More as well. You can adjust the notification settings from here as necessary.

When the phone is picked up, the gadget can be set to vibrate to alert you to missed calls and messages. You may access this by opening the Quick settings panel by swiping down from the top of the screen, then tapping the Settings button.

Choose Motions and gestures from the Advanced features menu. To activate it, simply tap the switch next to Alert when phone picked up.

Notably, tablets are not compatible with this.

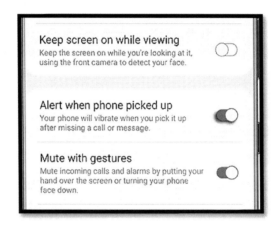

Dolby Atmos: When playing content, take pleasure in Dolby Atmos audio quality. You may access this by opening the Quick settings panel by swiping down from the top of the screen, then tapping the Settings button. Then select Sound quality and effects after selecting Sounds and vibration. Choose Dolby Atmos or Dolby Atmos for gameplay after that.

A headset or a pair of Galaxy Buds may be required to use this feature.

With a Galaxy phone, the alert is activated when the phone is picked up.

Equalizer: Choose a preset for your audio system that is tailored to a particular musical genre, or adjust the settings yourself. You may access this by opening the Quick settings panel by swiping down from the top of the screen, then tapping the Settings button.

Then select Sound quality and effects after selecting Sounds and vibration. For a music genre selection, tap Equalizer.

Improve the audio resolution of music and films for a clearer listening experience with UHQ upscaler. You may access this by opening the Quick settings panel by swiping down from the top of the screen, then tapping the Settings button. Then select Sound quality and effects after selecting Sounds and vibration. Choose an upscaler choice by tapping UHQ.

Notice that the Galaxy Buds models do not support this feature. Only approved Bluetooth devices and wired headsets can use it.

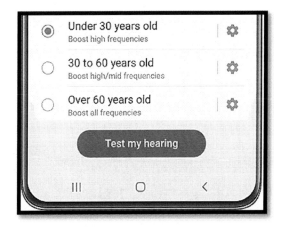

To improve your listening experience, adjust the sound to each ear individually. You may access this by opening the Quick settings panel by swiping down from the top of the screen, then tapping the Settings button. Then select Sound quality and effects after selecting Sounds and vibration. To choose when to adjust the sound settings, tap Adapt sound and then tap Adapt sound for. Afterwards, tap the sound profile that best suits you. Next, click the Settings button to edit it.

To have your device choose the ideal sound for you, tap Test my hearing.

List of Galaxy phone sound settings
Different app sound: Selecting an app to play media sounds on a Bluetooth speaker or headset apart from the other noises is an option (like notifications). You may access this by opening the Quick settings panel by

swiping down from the top of the screen, then tapping the Settings button. After selecting Sounds and Vibration, select Separate App Sound. Toggle Separate app sound on by tapping Turn on now, and then customize App and Audio device settings.

To use the audio settings, a Bluetooth device must be connected.

Do not disturb: While this mode is activated, you can prevent sounds and notifications. Additionally, you may define exceptions for specific individuals, applications, and alarms and create a timetable for repeating activities like meetings or sleep. You may access this by opening the Quick settings panel by swiping down from the top of the screen, then tapping the Settings button. Do not disturb should be selected after Notifications. You can specify preferences for Do Not Disturb, How Long, Sleeping, and Create a calendar, hide notifications, add calls, messages, and conversations, set alarms and sounds, and use apps.

Customize notifications from services and apps in advanced settings. In order to access this, swipe down from the top of the screen to reveal the Quick settings panel, then hit the Settings button. Next click on Advanced settings after selecting Notifications. Settings for Display notification icons, Display battery percentage, Notification history, Discussions, Floating notifications, Suggest actions and replies for notifications, Display snooze button, Notification reminders, App icon badges, and Wireless Emergency Alerts can all be customized.

CHAPTER ELEVEN

CONNECTION SETUP

We use Bluetooth to link Bluetooth earbuds, smartwatches, and other gadgets to our smartphones in the wireless technology era. Thus, multiple Bluetooth connections can be made simultaneously on modern devices. When your Samsung Galaxy S23 Ultra is paired with various Bluetooth connections, you can use two separate headsets at once.

However, your device's Bluetooth must be activated and capable of discovering or detecting other devices before you can transmit data or connect to devices. This guide will demonstrate how in a few straightforward stages.

By easily following the steps below to turn on Bluetooth on your Samsung Galaxy smartphone, you can connect the devices.

❖ Go to the Settings Menu.

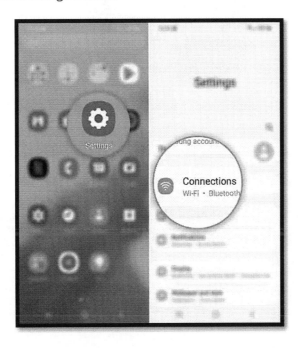

❖ Choose "Connections."
❖ Go to the Samsung Galaxy's main menu and choose "Connections."

❖ Choose "Bluetooth" by tapping it.

❖ To activate Bluetooth, click on it.

Four available or connected devices

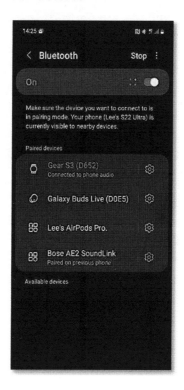

❖ Now, you can view every Bluetooth device that is prepared for pairing.

❖ In this page, all of the "Available Devices" and all of the "Paired devices" that you have previously connected to are displayed.

❖ To pair a device, tap its name.

❖ Choose the device you wish to associate your Samsung Galaxy S23 ultra with by tapping on its name.

❖ It should connect shortly after that.

How to Connect a Samsung Galaxy Smartphone to a Smart Gadget

In addition to the Settings menu, your Samsung Galaxy phone can be linked using Smart Things. You can immediately access a device from the SmartThings app if it has Bluetooth and is supported by SmartThings.

How to Connect Several Devices Using Bluetooth

By doing the following, you can use your phone to link to several devices via Bluetooth:

Bluetooth icon: Touch and hold

- ❖ Using the first method's Steps 1-3, scroll down from the top of your screen to find the Quick Settings Panel. Switch on Bluetooth, then tap and hold to see the currently accessible Bluetooth devices.
- ❖ Tap the gadgets you want to link.
- ❖ To connect many devices at once, click on the names of the Bluetooth devices that are listed as being available.

Finished media

- To listen to two headsets at once, return to the Quick Settings Panel and choose "Media output." If you do, a circle will appear next to each Bluetooth audio device you've connected.
- Examine the checkboxes next to the gadgets.
- By selecting the proper boxes for each device, you can play the same content on all of them at once.

Disable Bluetooth Pairing: How to Do It Upon completion of your work

It's a good idea to turn off Bluetooth when you're done using your Bluetooth-enabled devices in order to conserve battery life.

- To disable Bluetooth, open Settings, choose Connections, and then Bluetooth. Just press the top switch to turn Bluetooth off.
- Alternatively, you can use two fingers to slide downward from the top screen to enter the Quick settings window.
- Clicking the Bluetooth icon there will turn it off.

153

Activate or deactivate NFC on the Samsung Galaxy S23 Ultra.

Near field communication allows data to be transmitted between objects that are a few millimeters apart, typically back-to-back (NFC). Apps dependent on NFC must have NFC enabled in order to work properly.

- To access the applications screen from a Home Screen, swipe up from the screen's middle.
- These guidelines only apply to Standard mode and the Home Screen's default configuration.
- Go on Settings, Settings icon, Connections, and then select NFC and contactless payments.
- Toggle NFC and contactless payments on or off by tapping the corresponding icons in the upper right corner.

How to activate and deactivate Airplane Mode on S23 Ultra devices

A smartphone's airplane mode is an underappreciated luxury. Users can use airplane mode for a variety of significant purposes.

A user may choose to activate airplane mode for a variety of reasons. Some of the causes are as follows:

- ➤ When a complete shutdown of wireless services is required.
- ➤ If your battery is low, turning off internet-related apps and features.
- ➤ When you need to momentarily turn off features that might interfere with flight operations when you are really flying.

Longer Battery Life

Quickly powering a phone.

The Airplane setting can then be used for a variety of purposes. Flight mode can be turned on or off with relative ease. There are two approaches to taking care of it, and both require easy steps. The best feature of Airplane mode is that it removes the need for frequent phone activation and deactivation. By pressing a button, your phone goes into a partially awake state while still running any internet-independent applications.

On the screen of your device, swipe downward

- ➢ Your phone's screen should be on. To access the Quick Settings menu, slide down the screen from top to bottom.
- ➢ Tap the airplane symbol.
- ➢ On the quick settings menu, there should be a flight icon (which resembles a plane); if not, expand the menu area.

ON/OFF SWITCH FOR THE AIRPLANE MODE

- ➢ Airplane mode can be activated by tapping the flight icon once, and it can be deactivated by tapping it once more.
- ➢ Yep, activating and deactivating Airplane mode is that easy.

Using the Settings menu's Airplane mode

Going straight to settings and finding features is the best option if, for some reason, you can't find the flying icon in the quick settings menu or if you're a new user who doesn't know where particular features are placed.

Hence, if you wish to activate and deactivate Airplane mode through settings, refer to the detailed instructions below:

- ➢ Drag the screen of your phone downwards.
- ➢ Swipe up and down on your S23 ultra.
- ➢ Choose Settings.

155

> Locate and tap on the "Settings" icon.

Triple Tap Connections
> Choose Connections from the Settings menu after navigating there.
> Click "Airplane mode"
> Tap it to enable Airplane mode.
> To turn it off once more, repeat the procedure.

MOBILE NETWORK SETTING

1. After a factory reset or the first time you power on the device, you will be guided through a series of prompts to set up your device. Choose Start to proceed after selecting the preferred language.

2. To examine the device's policies, select Terms and Conditions, Privacy Policy, Transmission of Diagnostic Data, or Information Linking as requested. Choose Next after choosing the desired circles if you agree.

3. To set up using a different device, choose the chosen device and then adhere to the instructions. Choose Skip to proceed without utilizing another device.

4. To connect to a Wi-Fi network, choose the desired network name and adhere to the on-screen instructions. Choose Add network, then adhere to the instructions to connect to a hidden network. To move ahead without establishing a Wi-Fi connection, select Skip.

To continue setup without establishing a Wi-Fi connection and to disable Wi-Fi in order to preserve battery life, select Turn off Wi-Fi.

5. Choose Next and proceed as directed to complete the procedure if you want to transfer data from your old device to your new one in order to speed up setup. If you don't want to transfer your data, choose Don't copy.

6. If you want to utilize Google Services like the Play Store, Gmail, Google Maps, and more, you must log into a Google account.

Enter your email address or phone number and then follow the on-screen instructions to add your Google account. Choose Make account if you don't already have one but would want to. Choose Skip if you want to keep going without creating an account. Click Next to proceed.

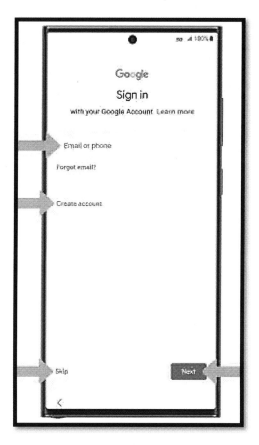

7. Look over the Google services prompt, then click the switches of your choice. After you're done, click Accept.

8. If you want to establish your screen lock right away, choose the desired choice and adhere to the setup instructions that appear on the screen. Choose Skip to continue without turning on device security features.

Reminder: If you choose Skip, you'll be asked to choose it again to confirm.

9. Look over the Google Assistant prompt before choosing I agree.

10. Read the prompt to subscribe to daily updates from the assistant, then click the relevant boxes. After finished, choose Next.

11. Go over any more apps you want to have downloaded to your smartphone when Wi-Fi is available, then check the boxes to the right of each one. When finished, click Ok.

12. Go through the Terms & Conditions prompt before choosing Next.

13. Examine the offer for AT&T Mobile Network Diagnostics, then click Agree.

14. To sign in to your Samsung account, enter the email address or phone number connected to your Samsung account, then click the arrow. After entering your password, click the arrow once more. Complete setup by following the instructions. If you do not already have a Samsung account, click Create account and proceed as directed by the setup instructions on the screen. Choose Skip to continue if you don't want to create a Samsung account.

15. Click Complete to finish the setup.

DATA USAGE
Analyze data use

1. From the Notification bar, swipe down and choose the Settings icon.

2. Choose Data consumption after choosing Connections.

3. Choose Cellular data usage. Data use for mobile devices will be shown.

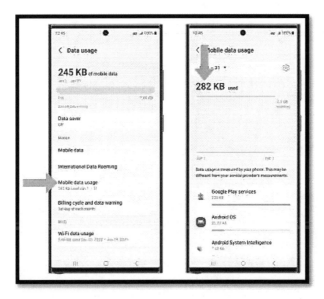

Analyze data usage by app

Scroll down the Mobile data use screen to see data usage by application.

Note: Swipe down from the notification bar, pick the settings icon, and then select Connections > Data usage > Data saver > Switch on now. This will prevent apps from using data while they are operating in the background.

Alter the billing cycle that is shown

Choose the Data consumption cycle drop-down menu from the Mobile data usage screen, then choose the desired billing period.

Decide on a data limit or warning.

1. Click on the Settings icon on the Mobile data usage screen.

2. Choose the preferred choice.

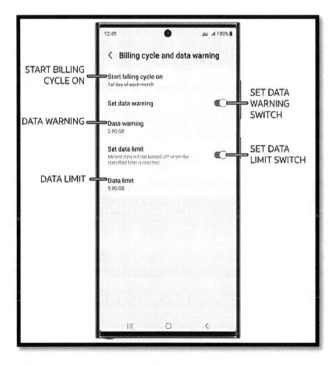

Choose Start billing cycle on under SET BILLING CYCLE START.

- **SET DATA WARNING:** Click this switch to enable or disable data warning.

- **SET DATA WARNING:** Choose Data warning when the Data warning switch is on.

Choose the Set data limit switch to enable or disable the data limit.

- **SET DATA LIMIT:** Click Data limit if the Data limit button is on.

When the mobile data limit is functional and has been reached, the mobile data block will continue to be in place until the device is manually configured to enable mobile data again, the limit threshold is raised, or a new data consumption cycle starts.

MOBILE HOTSPOTS

You can tether or use mobile hotspots to share your internet connection with additional devices. Many features and settings can also be customized to keep your hotspot private.

Suggestions for using a mobile hotspot

- ➢ Battery life and data allotment will be depleted when using the mobile hotspot.
- ➢ When a mobile hotspot is turned on, Wi-Fi is turned off.
- ➢ Your device's apps will utilize the mobile hotspot's data service while it is active.

Enable mobile hotspot

To activate the Mobile Hotspot feature on your Samsung phone or tablet, follow the instructions below.

Through Connection Preferences

1. Go to Settings > Connections.

2 Touch Tethering and Mobile Hotspot.

3 To turn this setting on or off, toggle Mobile Hotspot on or off.

via Quick Settings

1 To access your quick settings, swipe down from two locations at the top of the screen.

2 Touch Mobile Hotspot to enable or disable it.

Set Up A Mobile Hotspot

You can conceal your device and make other adjustments if you don't want unauthorized users to access your hotspot.

The configuration of a hotspot connection on your device is shown here.

1 Find and choose Mobile Hotspot and Tethering from the Settings menu.

2 Click on Mobile Hotspot.

3 Choose the three dots symbol found under your mobile hotspot settings.

After making changes to the Network name, Security, and Password, click Save.

There will be the following settings available:

Network name See and modify the hotspot's name.

Stow my gadget: Bypass others' ability to detect your phone or tablet.

Security: Choose the hotspot's level of security.

Password: See and modify your hotspot's password.

energy-saving mode Use mobile hotspot traffic analysis to lower battery consumption.

Protected management frames: Enables encryption of the hotspot.

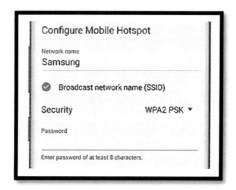

Mobile hotspot timeout settings

Your mobile hotspot will automatically turn off to conserve battery if no devices are connected for a predetermined period of time.

1 Find and choose Mobile Hotspot and Tethering from the Settings menu.

2 Click on Mobile Hotspot.

3.Choose the three dots icon under Mobile Hotspot Settings.

4.Click on Timeout Settings. Choose the amount of time to wait before shutting off your mobile hotspot if no devices are connected.

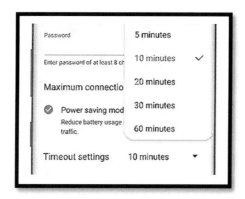

CHAPTER TWENTY

LOCK SCREEN AND SECURITY

A screen lock can be a great way to increase the protection of your phone. This prevents anyone besides you from accessing your phone. To make unlocking your phone easier, you can use a variety of lock methods, such as fingerprint recognition, patterns, and PINs.

Depending on the specific device you're using, there are different lock choices. Choose your preferred security technique from those that work with your device.

Where can I change how my devices operate?

You may be able to locate the lock screen settings there, depending on the specific device you are using. On the most recent smartphones, these choices can be located under Settings > Lock screen > Screen lock type.

Create a Simple Screen Lock Swipe to and tap Lock screen Settings. Then, hit Screen lock type and choose the lock type you want. To configure it, adhere to the on-screen directions.

These are the standard forms of screen locks:

Swipe the screen to make it unlocked.

• **Pattern:** You can unlock a screen by drawing a pattern on it.

• **PIN:** To unlock the screen, choose a PIN.

• **Password:** Set one up to allow you to unlock the screen.

No screen lock is present.

Install Biometric Security

You may configure your phone's biometric security so that you can use your face, your fingerprints, or even your eyes to unlock it! For the highest level of protection, Intelligent Scan combines face and iris recognition.

> ➢ Swipe to and tap Lock screen in Settings.
> ➢ Then, hit Screen lock type and choose the lock type you want. Then, adhere to the on-screen instructions after tapping the slider next to the option you want.

The following are the most basic biometric options:

> ➢ With your fingerprints, you may unlock the screen.

Face: Unlock your phone using facial recognition technology.

> ➢ The screen may be unlocked by using iris recognition.
> ➢ For improved accuracy and security, use an intelligent scan that combines face and iris recognition.

Safe Lock Configurations

> ❖ **Make Pattern Visible -** Toggle the entry of your unlock pattern to show or hide it.
> ❖ **Lock Automatically -** This lets you choose between an immediate lock timeout and a 30-minute lock timeout for your device.

❖ **Lock instantaneously with the side key -** This enables you to quickly lock your smartphone by pressing the Power key.

❖ **Auto factory reset -** Your smartphone will be reset to factory default settings and all data, including downloaded apps and files, will be wiped after 15 unsuccessful tries to unlock it.

❖ **Lock network and security** — While your phone is locked, you can choose to keep the network and security-related features locked. This makes it much simpler to find and guard against theft or loss.

❖ **Display lockdown option:** This setting on the power button disables Smart Lock and notifications on the Lock screen.

Time, Date, and Alarm

Discover how to use the alarm clock and set the date and time on your smartphone.

Date and time should be set.

1. Start on the home screen, slide down from the Notifications bar, and then tap the Settings button.

2. Choose General management by scrolling to it.

3. After choosing Date and Time, deactivate Automatic Date and Time Switch.

4. Choose the preferred option to update the date or time. Make any necessary edits, then click Done.

Note: The option Set date was used for this tutorial.

Set a new time zone.

Choose Disable automatic time zone switching from the Date and Time panel. Choose your desired time zone by clicking on Time Zone.

Note: On the Choose time zone page, select Region, then choose the desired region to choose a timezone in a different region.

Setup an alarm.

1. To access the Applications tray, swipe up from the home screen's center and choose the Clock app.

2. Click the Add icon after choosing the Alarm tab. After choosing the desired alarm time and settings, click Save.

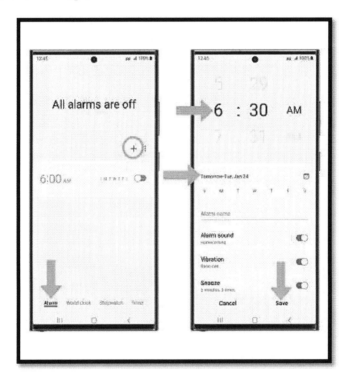

On/Off the alarm switch

To turn on or off the selected alarm, click the switch adjacent to it.

Eliminate an alarm

Choose Erase after selecting and holding the selected alarm.

Using the Sleep mode.

1. When you switch on sleep mode, your phone's screen automatically dims and is set to do not disturb while you are asleep. Swipe down from the Notifications bar on the home screen, then tap the Settings icon. Choose Sleep, then choose Modes and Routines.

Note: To start using Sleep mode for the first time, choose Start.

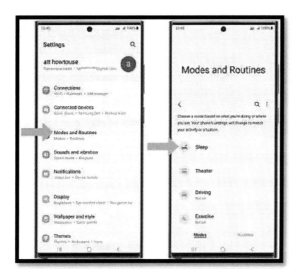

2. Choose Next after adjusting the time and making any necessary scheduling edits.

3. Edit Choose Next after setting the desired Do Not Disturb mode.

Note: Choose Skip to continue without configuring the do not disturb settings.

4. Adjust the parameters for the sleep mode as desired, then click Done.

Note: Choose Skip to continue without configuring the sleep mode.

5. Choose Turn on to manually activate the Sleep mode.

Note: Choose Switch off to exit Sleep mode.

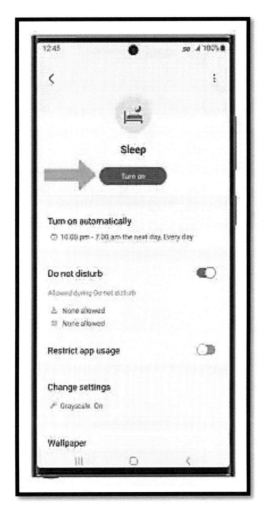

CHAPTER THIRTEEN

BIOMETRICS AND SECURITY

Fingerprint Security.

Fingerprint recognition, which takes advantage of your fingerprints' unique characteristics, increases the protection of your device. A fingerprint unlocks your phone more quickly and conveniently than a PIN or password. For fingerprint recognition to function, your fingerprint data must be stored and registered on your device.

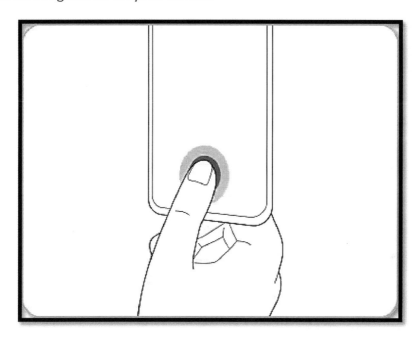

Note: Avoid using the fingerprint feature while submerged in water. Even if the device is IP68-certified, underwater use of the gadget prevents fingerprint recognition.

How to sign up with your finger

Step 1: Open the Settings app and select Biometrics and security.

Step 2: Click Fingerprints.

Step 3. After reading the instructions on the screen, select Proceed.

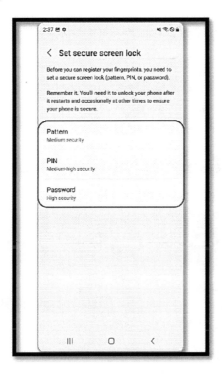

Step 4. Configure a safe screen lock technique.

Step 5: Apply pressure to the fingerprint recognition sensor using your finger.

Lift your finger up and reapply it to the fingerprint recognition sensor when the gadget has detected it. Continue doing this until the fingerprint is correctly registered.

For More Accurate Fingerprint Recognition

When you use this feature to detect your fingerprints on the device, the following conditions could interfere with its functionality:

It's conceivable that the device won't detect fingerprints with scars or wrinkles.

Note: The device might not be able to read the fingerprints from small or thin fingertips.

• To enhance identification performance, register the fingerprints of the fingers that are used to control the device the most.

• Your device's screen has a built-in fingerprint recognition sensor in the lower center.

• Check to make sure that nothing will scratch or damage the touchscreen area that houses the fingerprint identification reader, including coins, keys, pencils, necklaces, and other objects.

• Ensure that your fingertips and the area where the fingerprint recognition sensor is located in the middle of the screen's bottom are both dry and spotless.

The system might not recognize your fingerprint if you bend your finger or use a fingertip. Your fingertip should extend across the large surface of the fingerprint identification area as you press the screen.

Use of fingerprint identification

Use your fingerprints to unlock the screen

A pattern, PIN, or password are not required to unlock the screen; instead, your fingerprint can be used.

Step 1: Click Biometrics and security > Fingerprints on the Settings screen.

Step 2: Use the pre-programmed screen lock method to unlock the screen.

Step 3: To turn on the Fingerprint unlock switch, tap it. Put your finger on the fingerprint recognition sensor on the lock screen to have it scan your fingerprint.

Displaying The Fingerprint Icon

When you tap the screen while the screen is off, you can configure the device to display or conceal the fingerprint recognition icon.

Step 1: Click Biometrics and security > Fingerprints on the Settings screen.

Step 2: Use the pre-programmed screen lock method to unlock the screen.

Step 3: Choose an option and tap Show symbol when screen is off.

Erasing Recorded Fingerprints

It's possible to remove registered fingerprints.

Step 1: Click Biometrics and security > Fingerprints on the Settings screen.

Step 2: Use the pre-programmed screen lock method to unlock the screen.

Step 3: Choose the fingerprint you want to remove and tap Remove.

Despite the PIN, Pattern, Password release screen appearing if fingerprint recognition is enabled

According to Android OS policy, the screen that asks for your PIN, Pattern, or Password may still appear if you pick biometrics recognition, which includes utilizing Fingerprints or Face recognition to unlock your phone in some situations.

> - If, within the previous 24 hours, you used the device and unlocked it using biometrics like your fingerprints or facial recognition.
> - If 4 hours have passed since you last used your device's fingerprint or facial recognition to unlock it.
> - If your smartphone hasn't been unlocked using a PIN, pattern, or password for 72 hours and your fingerprint is configured as the screen lock type.
> - This is a response that is meant to increase the security of your device. Also, you can only unlock the screen using a PIN, Pattern, or Password after restarting the device or after leaving it idle for more than 24 hours.

If your phone doesn't detect your fingerprint right away

To reduce any temporary noise that might be produced when the screen is turned on or off, there is a 0.3 second delay before the relevant touch module is initialized. Therefore, if you attempt to use your fingerprint to turn on or off the screen right away, the device might not correctly detect it. After one more try, the feature should work.

If accidentally vibrating or unlocking while attempting to scan a fingerprint

Unintentional fingerprint recognition can be avoided by disabling the Fingerprint always on feature. If the function is activated, your phone will attempt to scan your fingerprint as long as you are holding it. Unwanted unlocks or noises could happen.

Use the instructions below to turn off the function if you find it cumbersome to use:

Step 1: Open the Settings app and select Biometrics and security.

Step 2: Click Fingerprint.

Step 3: Disable the switch next to "Fingerprint always on" in Step 2.

Note: Depending on the model and software version of the device, the screenshots and menus may differ.

If you've recently applied a new film or glass screen protector, you might need to re-register your fingerprint. Use the highest central portion of your fingerprint or the area with the greatest degree of curvature when registering or scanning your fingerprint.

The fingerprint identification feature could not function effectively if the surface of the protective film or glass screen protector has patterns, protrusions, dots, etc., or if you use a third-party product that is not approved for compatibility. Before to use, it is important to verify compatibility or recognition accuracy.

FACE IDENTIFICATION

Configure Facial Recognition

Note: You must first set a PIN, Pattern, or Password in order to activate Face recognition.

> ➤ One of your best security tools is your face because it is specific to you.

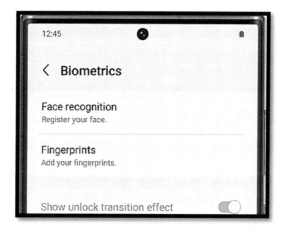

> ➤ Swipe to Security and privacy under Settings, hit that, then tap Biometrics to access this feature.
> ➤ After selecting Face recognition, enter your PIN or password. You must configure a secure screen lock if you don't already have one.
> ➤ While you hold the phone 8 to 20 inches away and place your face inside the circle, tap Continue.
> ➤ Maintain the position until the 100% mark appears on the progress meter. To complete the process, you might be asked to take off your spectacles.
> ➤ When you're done, make the required adjustments.

A word used in biometrics is facial recognition.

Now, a quick glance at your phone can open it! The following situations, though, might prompt your screen to request a PIN, pattern, or password if you've set up your lock screen to use facial recognition:

If the device hasn't been used for four hours, at least once per day, or if you've restarted it.

NOTE: You can keep your phone private by performing these additional verifications.

The following items will be accessible:

Facial detection alternatives

You can access additional protection settings and options after registering your face with your device. To access these options, select Settings and then click Protection and privacy. After choosing Biometrics, Facial recognition, and then Biometrics, enter your security details.

- **Erase face data:** Delete any previously stored facial recognition information.
- To improve recognition, add a different appearance. This is helpful if you adjust your makeup, facial hair, or hairdo.
- **Face Unlocks:** When your face is identified, your device unlocks.
- **Stay on the Lock screen until you swipe:** Even if you've already used Face recognition, stay on the Lock screen till you swipe.
- Eyes must be open for the device to recognize your face, adding an extra layer of security.

- Raise screen brightness momentarily to make it easier to see your face in the dark.

Tips on Face Recognition

✓ It doesn't get any simpler than that: simply show your face to unlock your device. Here are some tips for facial recognition if you're experiencing trouble.

✓ The process of identification can be impacted by eyeglasses, caps, masks, makeup, bangs, and beards. Changing your appearance can improve the device's ability to identify you in various settings.

✓ Make sure the camera lens is clean and that you are in a well-lit area.

✓ Make sure your image is not fuzzy for optimum effects.

✓ Compared to patterns, PINs, iris scans, and fingerprints, face recognition is less secure.

✓ Keep in mind that someone who resembles you could open your device (such as a twin).

✓ You can remotely unlock your handset using Find My Mobile and other techniques if you're experiencing problems doing so.

Try face registration once more if you are having trouble unlocking with face recognition. Open Settings, select Security and privacy, and then delete the existing facial data. Enter your credentials after selecting Facial recognition under Biometrics. Now that the facial recognition data has been cleared, you can start over by tapping Erase face data.

DIGITAL WELLBEING

A feature called "Digital Wellbeing" displays an app dashboard where users can see how long each application was open. By sliding to different pages, users may also view breakdowns by day, by hour, and by app.

View The Apps Dashboard
1.After selecting Settings, select Digital wellbeing.

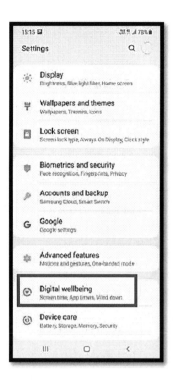

2. Press Dashboard.

3.Selecting an app's screen time, notifications received, and times opened requires a tap.

4. Review the list of apps based on the necessary option that was chosen.

Reduce Feature

To lessen eye strain before bed and avoid having your sleep interrupted, turn on Wind down mode.

Greyscale: Represents colors on a screen as shades of grey.

Don't be bothered: Except for permitted instances, set the device to muffle incoming calls and notification noises.

Please adhere to the instructions below to enable the Wind down feature:

1 Click Digital Wellbeing under Settings.

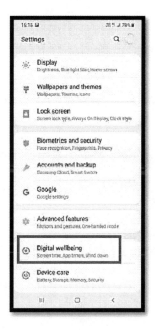

2 CLICK "Wind down."

PARENTAL CONTROL

With parental controls offered by Google's Family Link app, you can establish guidelines for how a phone or tablet should be used, enabling you to supervise your child's online learning and entertainment. As long as they are using software version One UI 2.0 or later, you can configure parental controls.

Setup a Samsung account for your child.

By providing your child a Samsung Account, you can manage the apps to which they have access. You can ban specific applications that you find offensive.

- After launching Settings and going there, tap your Samsung account's name.
- Select Family, Add Family Person, and Create Child Account, and then click Next.
- When you select Invite someone, a QR code, email, or Samsung account ID can be used to send the request. Please see the section after this for more details.
- After that, select Next to review the Child Privacy Disclosure to Parents.
- To accept, click.
- Choose an option on the following page, and then tap Accept to confirm your decision.
- Then you must input the credit card security code.
- Select Verify.

Note: To register a credit card with your Samsung account if you haven't already, press Register card and then adhere to the on-screen directions.

- Provide the details for your child, including their email address, password, name, and birthdate.
- Choose Create account.

- The verification code that was supplied to your child's email address must now be entered. To create your child's account, press Verify; after that, tap Next.
- Examine the details of SmartThings Discover. Tap Skip for this example.

Note: If desired, tap Next to continue configuring SmartThings Locate.

You can choose your child's account and control the apps they have access to from this point. You can select Permitted apps and then select the switch(es) next to the apps you don't want them to use, for instance. Tap Block when you're finished.

Put parental controls in place

- You can restrict your child's access to particular applications by configuring parental controls through the Google Family Link app.
- After you've done this, you'll be able to restrict their access to particular applications and keep track of how much time they spend on their phone or tablet.
- After opening Settings and moving there, tap Digital Wellbeing and parental settings.

- Tap Get started after selecting Parental controls.
- Depending on the user of the device, choose Child, Teen, or Parent. Tap Parent if that's the case.
- Install Google Family Link by tapping Get Family Link after that.

- Install the app if necessary. Once it has finished downloading, select Open to inspect the contents before selecting Get going.
- Choose your preferred Google account if more than one have been added to your device.
- You must then decide whether a parent, child, or teen will use the gadget. Tap Parent for the illustration.
- Choose Next after making sure the device you want to monitor is close. Tap I'm ready after reading the provided information.
- Depending on whether your child has a Google account, choose Yes or No. Tap Yes for this illustration.
- Go over the setup instructions with your child, then touch Done, followed by OK.

Download Google Family Link for kids & adolescents on your child's device, and then enter the Family Link setup code that is provided.

❖ To complete the connection between the two devices, follow the on-screen directions on each one.

❖ Once everything is set up, you can monitor everything using the Family Connect app. Tap Need support? for more information on how to operate the supervision features on Android or Chrome OS devices, see the instructions at the bottom.

❖ Open the app and select Add (the plus sign) from the menu in the upper right corner if you ever wish to add another youngster to supervise. The process is then repeated to add your child's Google account.

Give up monitoring an account

❖ Keep in mind that until your child reaches the age of 13, you must continue to monitor their account.

❖ Access to age-restricted content on Google's services may still be prohibited.

❖ Open the Google Family Connection app on the parent device.

❖ The child's account that you are no longer in charge of must be tapped.

❖ Choose Manage from the Settings menu, then select Account info.

❖ To ensure that you understand how halting monitoring would affect your child's access, tap Stop supervision and then follow the on-screen instructions.

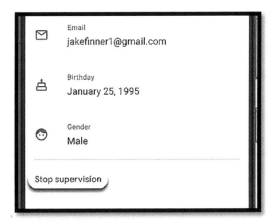

❖ After checking the option, select Cease supervision. Observe the directions that are given.

SET UP SAMSUNG PASS

Eventually, you won't need to remember a variety of login credentials and passwords for websites and apps. Samsung Pass employs biometric information, such as your fingerprints or irises, to verify your identity and protect your accounts.

Configure Samsung Pass.

➢ To use Samsung Pass, you must be logged into your Samsung account.

➢ Do you wish to log in using the fingerprint reader on your phone? When configuring Samsung Pass, your fingerprint information might be registered.

➢ You may also be able to scan your iris on some gadget types to verify your identity.

➢ Swipe to Security and privacy under Settings, then press Samsung Pass.

➢ After selecting Continue, sign in using your Samsung account information.

To configure your biometric information, tap Proceed. Choose Pattern, PIN, or Password, and then adhere to the instructions.

There will also be a choice to utilize iris identification if your device has an iris scanner.

➢ After that, you must register your fingerprint. Tap Done after completing the instructions.

➢ Your biometric information can now be used to sign into Samsung Pass.

➢ Change your network connection if you encounter problems installing Samsung Pass, get errors, or see a warning saying that service is temporarily unavailable.

➢ Instead, disable WiFi and solely use mobile data.

Utilizing Samsung Pass

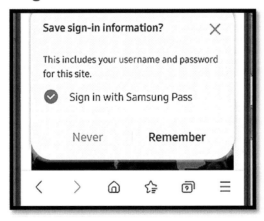

➢ You may now sign into websites and applications using Samsung Pass.

➢ Go to your preferred website using Samsung Internet and sign into your account there.

➢ Samsung Pass will ask you if you want to save the account details when you log into your account.

➢ Choose Remember. The next time you log in, all you have to do is scan your biometrics rather than entering your account details.

➢ Save login data in the Samsung Pass popup window.

➢ Remember that only Samsung Internet and other approved apps are compatible with Samsung Pass.

Activate and deactivate Autofill

When logging onto one of your accounts, you may be asked to utilize your biometric information if Samsung Pass is configured.

Use the Autofill service as follows:

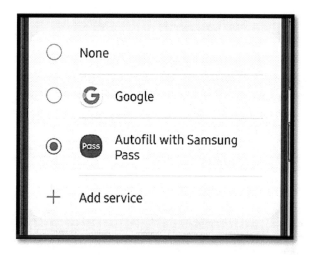

➢ Go to Settings, click General management, then select Passwords and autofill.

➢ Make sure Autofill with Samsung Pass is chosen after tapping Autofill with Samsung Pass.

You can choose Google as well, but we strongly advise using Samsung Pass because it is supported by Samsung Knox, a mobile security platform with military-grade security.

The option to use autofill with Samsung Pass on a Galaxy phone

Note: To stop using this service, perform the same actions but select None.

Disable Samsung Pass.

You don't want to use Samsung Pass anymore, do you? No problem, you can switch it off whenever you want. For security reasons, Samsung Pass will be reset to its default settings, and all related data (including biometric information) will be deleted.

- Under Preferences, swipe to Security and privacy, then tap Samsung Pass. Sign in when asked.
- After choosing Additional options, click Settings (the three vertical dots).
- Select the device you wish to uninstall from the list of all devices that support Samsung Pass, then tap Additional options (the three vertical dots).
- When you select Uninstall on the pop-up, all Samsung Pass data will be erased from that device and Samsung Pass will be reset.

- Open Samsung Wallet, then touch Menu to delete Samsung Pass from the app.

- Choose your desired device, then touch Settings, manage devices, then uninstall.
- To confirm, tap Delete once more.

Your phone stores everything, including confidential data and perhaps humiliating images. With a unique passcode, you can conceal your private information with Secure Folder. In this manner, nobody will view your collection of selfies.

Create A Secure Folder

- The Secure Folder option won't show up in the Biometrics and security settings menu if your device doesn't support it.
- A good security system in real life consists of numerous cameras and locks.
- Fortunately, setting up Secure Folder on your phone is a lot less complicated.

- Choose Settings, then select Biometrics and security, and finally select Secure Folder.
- Choose Continue.
- By tapping Proceed, the required permissions are granted.
- Tap OK after logging into your Samsung account if necessary.
- For access to Secure Folder, you will be required to configure a security measure such a PIN, password, or pattern.
- To configure your passcode and gain entry to your Secure Folder, simply follow the on-screen instructions.
- Then click OK.
- A notification to enable Reset with Samsung account will appear.
- In the event that you neglect your PIN, password, or pattern if this option is not enabled, you won't be able to access your secure folder.
- If you want to be able to retrieve your Secure folder, tap Activate.

Add applications or folders to the secure folder

You are hesitant to obtain your bank's app because you are worried that someone will steal your personal data. No one other than you will even be aware that the software is on your phone if you add it to Secure Folder.

- Tap Add applications after Secure Folder has been configured (the plus sign).
- To add an app to the folder, touch it, then tap Add.
- A copy of the program will be visible in your Secure Folder.
- Select the More choices button (the three vertical dots), then select Add files.

- Now, you can pick the kind of file you want or use My Files to search for any file on your computer.
- Files should be moved to a secure folder.

- Even when you aren't signed in, you can always upload images or files to your secure folder.
- Go to and launch a file-containing program, such as Gallery.
- To transfer a file into a secure folder, tap and hold it.
- After selecting More, select Transfer to Secure Folder.
- You can access the file in Secure Folder after it has been moved.
- Go to the marked Secure Folder on a Galaxy phone.
- To transfer files to a secure folder, they must first be saved to internal storage or an SD card.
- You cannot transfer files from your Dropbox account to a Secure Folder.
- Delete the items in the Secure Folder.

What if you want to share a movie or photo from your Secure Folder with a friend? Use My Items in Secure Folder is required.

❖ Visit and launch Secure Folder.
❖ If asked, enter the Secure Folder passcode information.
❖ Search for the item you want to remove from the Secure Folder by tapping My Files.
❖ Tap More after touching and holding the image. To exit the secure folder, select Transfer.
❖ Remove the highlighted Secure Folder choice from a Galaxy phone.
❖ The file will be transferred to a new folder in the Gallery and stored in your phone's internal storage if it was previously saved on your SD card.

Hide the Secured Folder

You can hide the Secure Folder from your phone's Apps interface if you don't want anyone to even know it's there.

1.Use two fingertips to swipe downward to reveal the Quick Settings panel. To hide or reveal the program, swipe to and tap Secure Folder.

2.As an alternative, you can access Preferences, select Biometrics and security, and then select Secure Folder. After logging in, swap the Add Secure Folder to Apps interface on or off by tapping the button next to it.

3.Highlighted on the Quick Settings screen is the Secure Folder symbol.

4.By altering the Secure Folder's name or symbol, you can keep it hidden. Open Secure Folder by navigating there, and when asked, enter your security information.

5.Tap Customize after tapping More choices (the three vertical dots). You can modify the app's name and symbol from this point. When finished, press Submit.

Access methods for Secure Folder

Whether you've hidden Secure Folder or simply want a different method to access it, there are a few ways to locate and open it. If you've lost your password, you can also reset your security credentials.

- Swipe down from the top of the screen with two fingers to uncover the Quick settings window and the Secure Folder icon.
- Enter your password details when prompted.
- You can also access the Secure Folder using these steps from your Apps screen; just open the Apps screen and select Secure Folder.
- From an app's user interface, **Select Secure Folder** after sliding up to show the Apps screen on the Home Screen.
- Enter your password details when prompted.
- Select Secure Folder from the drop-down menu under Biometrics and security in Options after opening that section of the menu.

- Enter your password details when prompted. Select Secure Folder from the Apps option to launch it.

You can easily reset your Secure Folder if you forget the security credentials if Reset with Samsung account is enabled. After launching the Private Folder, enter your Passcode, pattern, or password. If it's incorrect, tap the Forgot caution. Before logging into your Samsung account, select Refresh from the pop-up menu that displays.

Another PIN, pattern, password, or registered biometric will be presented to you for selection. To create your new security credentials, adhere to the directions displayed on the screen. You can now view Secure Folder once more.

You won't be able to regain access to your Secure Folder if Reset with Samsung Account was not activated when you established your security method.

Uninstall Secure Folder

- ➢ You can fully uninstall Secure Folder from your phone if you want to get rid of all of its data.
- ➢ Choose Settings, then select Biometrics and security, and finally select Secure Folder.
- ➢ After selecting More options, select Uninstall.
- ➢ After reading the details, tap Uninstall to approve.

CHAPTER FOURTEEN

GOOGLE APPLICATIONS

You can use a number of Google applications that are already preinstalled on your Galaxy phone and tablet. You can use Chrome to browse the web, Maps to find your way around, and YouTube to view your favorite videos, for example. The Google Play Store also offers additional apps.

Make use of Google apps

You might already have the following Google apps loaded on your smartphone. If they aren't already on your phone, you can download them from the Google Play Store.

To find your Google apps, swipe up from a Home page to show the Apps screen. Then, go to and touch the Google folder.

Chrome: Use the Chrome browser to explore the internet and sync your open tabs, bookmarked pages, and address bar information between your computer and mobile device.

- Drive lets you access files saved to your Google Drive cloud account and share, examine, and rename them.
- Make video conversations to your loved ones to meet up.

Gmail: Use Google's web-based email tool to send and receive emails.

On a Galaxy phone, a summary of the applications in the Google folder

Google: Use a search engine that recognizes your interests to find online material. You can enable your custom feed to get more material that is relevant to you.

Use your Android phone to make purchases at participating retailers and in mobile applications with Google Pay.

Use the Google TV app to view movies and TV shows that you have bought from Google Play. In addition, you can watch movies that you've saved

Access maps to find instructions and other location-based data. To use Google Maps, location services must be enabled.

Photos: Google Photos lets you instantly store and back up your photos and videos to your Google Account.

Messages: Chat features in Google's text messaging app let you share higher-resolution images, videos, and text over Wi-Fi.

YouTube: Use your device to watch and post YouTube videos.

Use Microsoft applications

Your smartphone might come with the following Microsoft apps already installed. You can download them from the Google Play Store or the Galaxy Store if they aren't already on your smartphone.

Swipe up on a Home Screen to reveal the Apps screen. From there, navigate to and select the Microsoft folder to locate your Microsoft apps.

Outlook: Use Outlook to access email, a schedule, contacts, tasks, and more. Additionally, the app can sync material from Microsoft 365, Gmail, Yahoo! Mail, and other services.

To use this function, you must link an Outlook account to your phone.

Connect and network with other people globally on LinkedIn. You can make a profile, look for employment possibilities, and see company updates.

a list of the Microsoft applications in the Galaxy phone's folder

Office: The Microsoft Office mobile software lets you use Word, Excel, and PowerPoint applications on your mobile device. You can format documents in Microsoft Office and present them to peers, family, and coworkers.

OneDrive: Create a free online OneDrive account to store and exchange documents, videos, and more. You can view OneDrive from a desktop computer, tablet, or mobile device.

Link to Windows: Using Your Phone and Link to Windows, you can move files between your computer and phone. Additionally, you can utilize your mobile applications on a PC.

CHAPTER FIFTEEN

APPLICATIONS USAGE

Some applications will already be installed on your new device when you turn it on for the first time. Some of these programs can't be disabled or deleted because they are required for your device to function properly.

Some apps can be disabled but cannot be uninstalled. This is because they are advantageous for your smartphone's everyday use and core functions.

Any independently purchased app may well be uninstalled

Only the entire application can be removed from your phone. Disabling an app prevents it from running in the background and removes it from the apps interface. Disabled applications won't receive any more updates.

Depending on where you bought your device, it might come with a variety of preloaded apps. For instance, if you purchase a device from a cell network, it might come pre-installed with their apps.

You can deactivate or uninstall applications from the apps screen.

1.You can rapidly ascertain whether you can disable or uninstall an app through the apps page.

Swipe up from the home screen to get to the apps tab.

2 In your hands, hold the icon of the application you wish to disable or uninstall.

3.If it's feasible to uninstall the application, this option will be available in the menu.

4 If there is only a disable choice available and the app cannot be uninstalled,

5 If it is impossible to disable or uninstall the app, neither of these choices will be available.

Through the settings menu, remove or deactivate apps.

1 From the home screen, swipe up and select the Settings symbol.

2 Select "Apps" 3 Select "the program you want to disable or remove"

3 The choices will vary depending on the app. The choice to Uninstall will be available if the app can be deleted.

4 There will be a Disable option if the app cannot be deleted but is not required for device operation.

5 The Disable option will be grayed out if the app cannot be deleted but is required for device functionality.

Through the apps screen, remove or deactivate applications.

Through the apps page, you can quickly determine whether you can disable or uninstall an app.

1 To access the apps page from the home screen, swipe up.

2 Hold the icon of the program you want to disable or uninstall in your hands.

3. This choice will show up in the menu if it's possible to uninstall the app.

4 Only the choice to disable will be available if the app can be disabled but not uninstalled.

5 If it is impossible to disable or uninstall the app, neither of these choices will be available.

LATEST APPS DOWNLOAD

Get a mobile app by downloading

1. From the home screen, select the Play Store application.

On the Google Play Store, you can discover the newest music, apps, games, videos, and other content. Gmail accounts are necessary for access. For more information or assistance, kindly consult the Google Play Help website.

2. Press the Explore key. Type the name of the desired program into the search box, then select a suggestion or hit the Search key. Select Configuration.

Note: If prompted, examine the permissions and click Accept only if you are in agreement. Apps made for Android 6.0 and later will ask you for authorization the first time you use them. Upon request, check the permissions, and if you're satisfied, select CONTINUE.

On Android 8.0 devices, a "TRY NOW" option will also be accessible, enabling users to make use of an app function without downloading the entire app.

3. The Notification bar will display a downloading icon while the material is downloading.

4. After the app has downloaded and been installed, choose Launch to launch it.

Reminder: Within 15 minutes of payment, apps may be returned. From the Play Store, choose Account > My apps & games > the chosen app > REFUND > YES to return the app.

App update

Select the Account icon from the Play Store, go to Manage Apps & Device, look for Updates, and then click Update next to the chosen app to update it, or click Update All to update all apps.

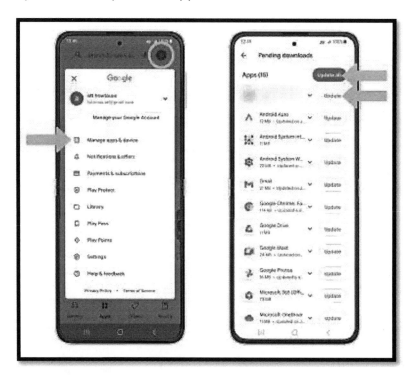

Uninstall an application

Choose and hold the chosen app in the Apps tray, then click App Info > Uninstall.

Note: To affirm, click OK. Select and hold the chosen app, then choose Remove from Home to remove it from the home screen.

Install the application again

Select Install from the chosen app's menu in the Play Store, then follow the on-screen instructions.

CHAPTER SIXTEEN

SAMSUNG CAMERA ULTILIZATION

Amazing camera features on the Galaxy S23 Ultra make it easy to capture still images, moving images, and photos. You can use the AI Image Enhancer to increase the resolution of your pictures, zoom in or out with a single touch, and even take pictures and videos in total darkness using the **Nightography** mode on the S23 Ultra series cameras. Additionally, the Gallery app can use your images to make personalized tales for you!

Night selfies and nighttime portraits

Photos taken with the Galaxy S23 ultra series' Nightography features will have stunning high quality and clear details.

- Open the Camera app by going there, then swipe to MORE and select it.
- After lining up your picture, tap NIGHT.
- By pinching the screen with your fingers or by tapping one of the available choices at the bottom of the screen, like 3x or 10x, you can zoom in and out.
- Click Capture.
- Alternately, you can select the front camera icon to change to it.
- For a picture, tap Capture.

A selfie video and a nighttime video

On your Galaxy S23 ultra series, advanced Nightography capabilities are also available when recording videos.

- The automatic super steady function will help you obtain smooth wide images when using Night video mode while moving.
- You can record group selfies with your friends using Night selfie videos.
- Go there and choose VIDEO to launch the Camera application.
- Tap the icon for Night shot, which is a circle, to turn it on.
- After that, tap Start to begin recording.

Note: By pinching the screen with your fingers or tapping one of the options, such as 3x or 10x, at the bottom of the display, you can increase or decrease the size of the picture.

- You'll be given instructions on how to keep your hand posture steady while recording.
- Press Pause to end the recording.
- Alternatively, you can switch to the front camera by selecting that symbol.
- Tap Start to start a photo/video recording.

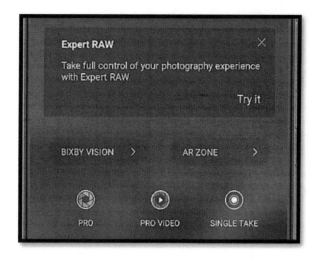

In the Gallery app, you can use the personalized stories option to review your past memories. Based on your photos and videos, an algorithm will recommend and automatically construct stories. Then, using carefully curated Spotify playlists, you can contribute your own background music to the stories!

With the Expert RAW app, which can be purchased from the Galaxy Store, the Galaxy S23 series can also take high-quality pictures.

SHOOTING MODES

The cameras on Galaxy phones and tablets have a number of shooting modes and camera settings, which make it simple to record and give your photos and videos personality. A few features of the camera include Portrait mode, Super slow-motion, Augmented Doodle, and Director's view. Changing the camera's available options, such as resizing the video or adding grid lines, will allow you to advance the situation.

Set up the shooting modes.

When taking photos or videos, choose from a variety of shooting modes to achieve the impact and appearance you desire.

➢ To launch the Camera app, swipe up from the bottom of your phone's screen to reveal the Apps menu.

➢ Swipe the app's screen right and left to switch between shooting settings. The following is a summary of the shooting options:
➢ Take several images and videos in one motion, from various perspectives.

Photo: Take photographs while letting the camera choose the best settings.

Record videos while letting the camera choose the best parameters for them.

More: Pick from the other firing options. To add or remove shooting settings from the tray at the bottom of the Camera screen, tap Add.

Pro: While shooting pictures, manually adjust the ISO sensitivity, exposure level, white balance, and color tone.

Panorama: By taking photos in either a horizontal or vertical orientation, you can produce a linear image.

Food: Use vivid hues to emphasize in your photographs.

Use this at night to capture pictures without a flash when it's dark outside.

Add and modify background effects for pictures in portrait mode.
Video in portrait mode: Add and modify backdrop effects.

Professional video: While recording videos, manually change the ISO sensitivity, exposure value, white balance, color tone, and mic sound settings.

Super slow motion: To capture movies with the best possible slow motion, shoot them at a very high frame rate. After recording a video, you can play a particular section in slow motion.

For watching in slow motion, record videos at a high frame rate.

Hyperlapse: Produce a time lapse movie by taking multiple frames-per-second recordings. Depending on the image being captured and the movement of the camera, the frame rate is altered.

Director's perspective: Use advanced features to focus on a specific object, switch between the back camera's lenses, and more.

Set up your shot after deciding on a shooting technique, then snap some photos or movies. Use Space Zoom to zoom in and get a closer view if your topic is far away.

CAMERA SETTINGS

The parameters for your camera can be customized using the settings menu. To launch the Camera app, swipe up from the bottom of your phone's screen to reveal the Apps menu. To access more options, select the Settings icon on the app.

Note: The settings you can use will rely on the features of your particular model.

Key Features

Scene optimizer: Adapt exposure, contrast, white balance, and other settings automatically based on what is seen in the camera screen. When using the back camera, the Scene Optimizer is the only option. When taking pictures of nature or in low light, the Scene optimizer icon will change automatically based on what the camera recognizes, such as a leaf when shooting outside or a moon when shooting inside. Additionally, you can display an icon for text and document scanning from the back camera.

For assistance lining up great shots, use the on-screen guides.

Scan QR codes: The camera automatically recognizes QR codes.

Pictures

➢ When you swipe the shutter button to the closest border, you can decide whether to capture a burst of pictures or make a GIF.
➢ Create a stamp and add it to your pictures.
➢ The data that the stamp contains can also be chosen.
➢ You have the choice of saving images in the HEIF or RAW formats.

High-efficiency images: Save photos in this format to free up room on your phone. Some apps and sharing websites might not accept this format.

Save JPEG and RAW copies of any photos you capture in Pro mode.

Ultra-wide shape correction: Automatically fix images captured with an ultra-wide lens that have been distorted.

ALBUM CREATION

Use your phone or tablet to relive all those priceless memories rather than that cumbersome picture album that you left at home.

You can watch, edit, and manage your photos, videos, and albums directly on your Galaxy device using the Gallery app.

WATCH AND EDIT MOVIES AND IMAGES.

If you spent an hour trying to get the perfect picture or film, you can check out the results in the Gallery. Additionally, you have access to a wide range of filters, effects, and editing techniques for your photograph or video.

Navigate there to launch Gallery, then pick the Pictures option. To search for a specific image or video, tap the Search icon in the upper right corner. You can use a search to find something based on its tag, record name, or other details.

On more recent devices, the possibility exists to combine images with a similar aesthetic. When this occurs, a small number (i.e., 2, 3, or so on) will show in the corner of some image thumbnails rather than all of your images appearing in the Picture tab. To examine the grouped images, simply tap the thumbnail.

Simply press the Group similar images icon at the top of the screen if you don't want to use this feature and prefer to see all of your pictures (it looks like a square).

When you've located the image or video you want to see, tap the thumbnail to watch it. To access more choices, tap the More options button (the three vertical dots). You can print a picture, examine the file's details, make a picture your background, and more!

Create albums for your photos and videos.

Do you regularly record a special interest? Create a folder in the Gallery app for all of those pictures and videos so you can reach it later without having to scroll through all of your other pictures and videos.

Touch and hold an image or video to select it from the Pictures tab. Alternately, you can choose Modify by first choosing More options (the three vertical dots). Next, choose the picture(s) or movie you want (s).Tap More at the bottom of the page to continue. To move the image(s) or video(s) to another album, press Copy to album. You can also copy and transfer them into another album by selecting Move to album.

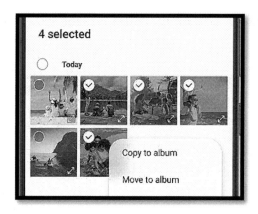

Next, choose the album you want to paste the picture(s) or video(s) into or transfer them to. They've been added to that album now.

Tap the Albums tab at the bottom to start a new collection.

At the top, click Add (the plus symbol). Enter the album name in the Album field, then press Create. Using the procedures outlined previously, you can transfer photos and videos to the new album.

Remove the photos and videos.

A fantastic photo or film was ruined by your friend. Remove their joke in a few simple steps.

> ➤ Tap Albums from the Gallery menu, then press the album you want to view.

➢ You can remove one or more photos or videos by touching and holding their thumbnail. After selecting Delete, affirm by selecting Move to Trash.

➢ Open Gallery and select Menu (the three horizontal lines) from the bottom to completely remove photos or videos from the Trash.

➢ After selecting Trash, select More choices (the three vertical dots).

➢ After selecting Empty, select Erase.

Album Creation

Your Gallery may become a little unorganized due to the abundance of pictures and videos. Simply make an album to purge the excess.

Tap the Albums tab in Gallery, then press Add (the plus sign). From the following music categories, you can choose:

BUILD A STANDARD ALBUM.

- Create a photo album that will automatically update with new images of the individuals you choose to include.

Group: Make a group first, then add songs to it. For more details, see the part after this one.

- Create a shared picture to make it available to others.
- Select a name for your new collection, then select Create.
- You can add images or movies to your new album if you selected a standard album. At the bottom, choose either Album or Photos.
- After choosing the images or movies you want to include, tap Done.

- Then, pick Copy or Move to decide how you want to move the images or videos.

SORT ALBUMS INTO GROUPS

❖ Once you've made a few albums, you can combine them to make it simpler to locate your pictures and videos.

❖ Tap the Albums tab in the Gallery, then tap Add (the plus symbol) at the top.

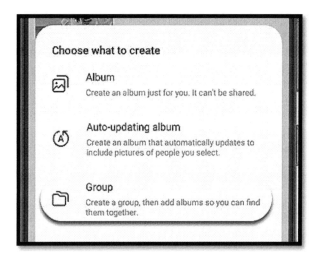

❖ Click Group.

❖ Tap Create after entering the intended name for your new group.

❖ Tap the group, then tap Add albums to add songs to your newly created group.

❖ Next, pick the songs you want.

❖ When you're done, tap Submit.

SHARE IMAGES AND VIDEOS.

Use Nearby Share, Quick Share, or Private Share to send your pals some fresh pictures or videos. Without opening any additional apps, you can use these features to transmit your photos and videos straight to a tablet or phone that is compatible.

You can post your photos and videos to your preferred apps, like Facebook or Instagram, by using the Sharing panel.

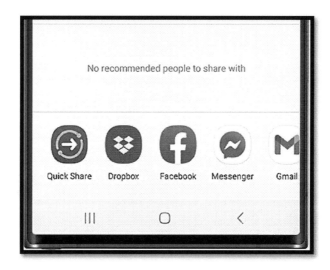

- ❖ Open Gallery and choose the image or video you want to share to get started.
- ❖ At the bottom of the page, click the Share icon.
- ❖ To share your picture or video, choose the app of your choice and then adhere to the on-screen directions.

TAKE TEXT OUT OF A VIDEO

You can extract and even duplicate text from videos in your Gallery if they have text in them. or distribute the content to others.

- ✓ Open the Gallery app by navigating there, then look for and choose a movie.
- ✓ When the video begins, press the pause button. after that, press the yellow T icon located to the right.
- ✓ Tap the words you want to extract after that. The circles can be used to pick more or less text.

After that, pick one of the following:

- ✓ To extract the text from the movie in the Gallery app, click the "T" icon.

Map: To find something that is stated in the video, use Google Maps.

Translate: To translate the text you chose from the movie, use Google Translate.

Copy: Add the text to the clipboard on your computer.

Choose all: Pick every word that appears on the screen.

Share: Distribute the written word. Pick a sharing choice after tapping Share.

CHAPTER SEVENTEEN

Gallery Settings

How to control your Gallery app's photos and videos by syncing them with OneDrive

You can submit each photo and video you own to a cloud storage service using OneDrive on your Galaxy phone. By configuring OneDrive and Gallery to automatically connect with one another, you can view your files whenever you want and access them again later from a PC with OneDrive or another mobile device.

How to link your MS and Samsung accounts using Cloud Sync

To connect your Gallery app with OneDrive, you must first sign up for an account there. You can access OneDrive on your Samsung phone through Cloud Sync even if you don't have a Microsoft account.

The stages are listed below:

Step 1: First, open the Gallery app. Next, select the Menu button at the bottom (it looks like three horizontal lines).

Step 2: Click on the Settings button.

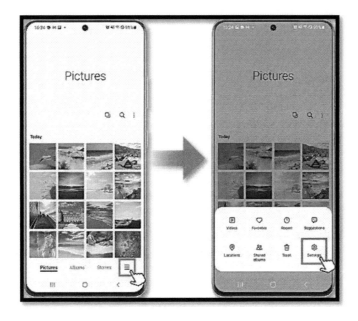

Step 3: In the Gallery settings section, select Cloud Sync.

Step 4: After reading the notification and accepting the permissions, tap Connect.

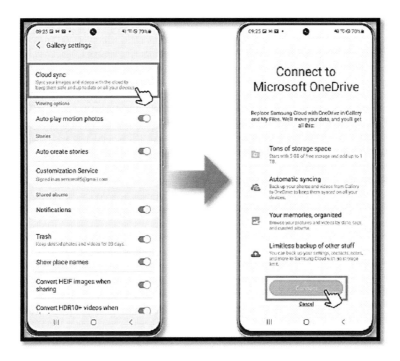

Step 5: Click the Connect icon.

Step 6: After selecting Create one!, link your existing Samsung account to a Microsoft account. Follow the in-app directions all the way through.

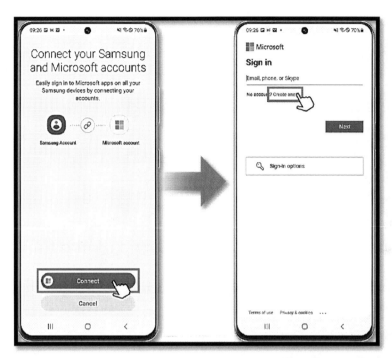

Note: Only when you have not yet signed in to OneDrive does the Cloud Sync menu show. When you are already signed in, the Sync with OneDrive menu will be visible. Make sure the Internet is accessible to you.

How to connect particular albums in the Gallery application
Family vacation pictures and group selfies with your closest friends are just two examples of the essential albums you can sync and save to OneDrive. The steps below should be followed beginning with the Gallery settings page.

Step 1: Select Sync with OneDrive

Step 2: To connect, tap Albums.

Step 3: Tap the switch next to an album to select which albums will connect with OneDrive.

How to get documents off OneDrive

You can download the pictures and movies that you have synced with OneDrive from a different phone, tablet, or computer.

Step 1: Launch the OneDrive application and select the Photos option.

Step 2: Tap the image or movie you want to download to your phone.

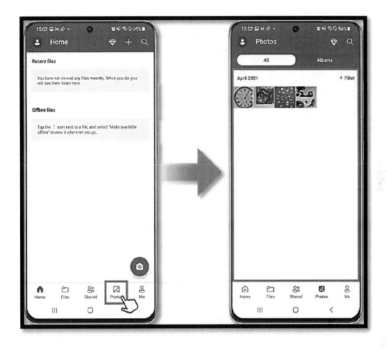

Step 3: Select Download from the menu.

Step 4: Tap SAVE once more to affirm. Tap the Back arrow icon to select a different place for your file, such as Documents or Pictures, if you'd like to save it somewhere else.

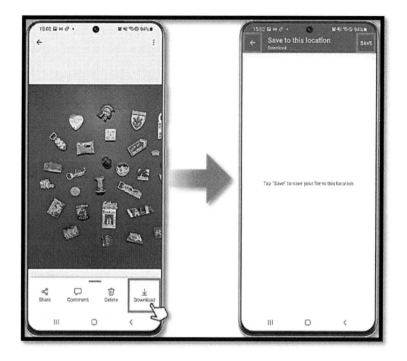

How to retrieve deleted OneDrive data

It won't be a big problem if you accidentally delete photos from OneDrive. Deleted photos and movies aren't immediately and permanently gone. They are kept in the trash bin for a few days so you can get your files from there. The OneDrive program's "Me" and "Recycle Bin" sections are where you can find the removed files.

How to synchronize your Gallery photos and videos with OneDrive right away

You can easily turn on the Gallery app's auto-sync function to sync all of your photos and videos to OneDrive even though it may be disabled by default. If you already have a OneDrive account, use the steps below.

1. First, open the Gallery app. Next, select the Menu button at the bottom (it looks like three horizontal lines).

2. Click on the Settings button.

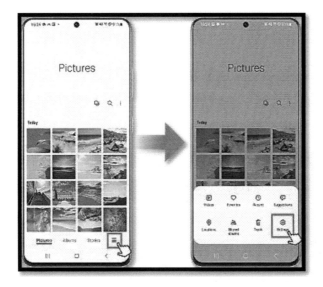

3. Tap the option to make Sync with OneDrive active. Your Gallery images and videos will instantly sync with OneDrive.

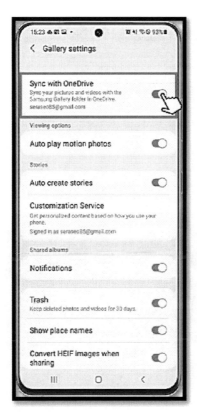

Note: Depending on the device model and program version, menus and screenshots may differ.

How to take a screenshot on the Samsung S23 Ultra

We go over the various methods for taking screenshots on the Samsung S23, S23+, and S23 Ultra in this video.

METHOD 1: Volume Down + Power Keys

This is a fairly straightforward method for taking a snapshot on the Samsung S23, and it has been used frequently for taking screenshots on Samsung phones for some time. Simply hold down the volume down key and the power key concurrently for one second, and your screenshot will appear.

✓ Hit both the power and volume down keys.

✓ On the edge of the Samsung S23 ultra, look for the power and volume down keys.

✓ For one second, simultaneously press the power key and the volume down key.

✓ It should be noted that if you press the keys for a prolonged period of time, the device will shut down.

✓ There will be a screenshot captured.

✓ You should be able to capture with your phone.

✓ Edit or trim the picture as desired.

Following the screenshot, a menu asking for additional changes like cropping the image or adding a drawing to the image will show.

Method 2: Utilize a Palm Gesture to take a picture on a Samsung S23.

One of the most elegant and beautiful snapshot methods ever. A smooth and simple method of capturing a screenshot is via palm gesture.

Furthermore, no button is required to capture this page! Let's examine how to accomplish it step-by-step.

▪ Open Settings

- From the top of the device, swipe down and select settings.

Two Sophisticated Functions

- Select "Advanced features" by scrolling down the list of choices.

Hand movements and motions

- Choose "Motions and gestures" from the list that appears.

Swipe your palm to photograph

- Turn on the "palm swipe to capture" switch; if it is already on, keep it on.

Make a left to right swipe.

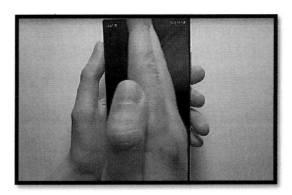

Using a light karate chop motion, position your hand sideways, pinky side down, on your screen to take a screenshot. Your phone will capture a screenshot if you swipe your palm in a left to right motion.

Greetings, Bixby!

Forget about not having to click any buttons; using your Samsung assistant Bixby, you won't even have to touch the screen to take a screenshot. Using vocal commands, you can direct your virtual assistant to take a screenshot on your behalf.

It is necessary to be signed into your Samsung account in order to use Bixby, so make sure you are. Once you've logged in, move on to the following stages.

1 Bixby app options

- Go to the Bixby app and access settings.

Vocal wake-up

- Activate the audio wake-up setting.

Select the thing you want to record.

- Navigate to the website or image you want to capture.

Take a picture, Bixby.

- Your virtual assistant will capture a screenshot for you if you say "Hi Bixby, take a screenshot."

Method 3: How to capture a longer/scrolling screenshot

There will be instances when you need a longer screenshot because you want to capture the entire page or a much larger image. Samsung also has your back in that regard. Any of the aforementioned techniques can be used to capture a lengthier screenshot.

Of course, you'll need to take extra measures for that, and we'll teach you how to do that.

Locate the edit button.

- An editable floating icon will show up on top of the image after it has been taken.

Press the two lines to the left.

- Select the box icon's two downward-pointing lines.

Down the screen, scroll.

- You can now scroll down the website and choose how long you want the screenshot to be.

Resize the photo.

- Once the image has been cropped to your preference, your lengthy screenshot is available.

You might not have given your phone the necessary authorization to take a screenshot, which is one of the main reasons it might not be taking one.

- ➢ Navigate to preferences and select "Apps."
- ➢ Choose the more options icon in the upper right corner of the "Apps" section.
- ➢ Select "Special entry" from the menu now.
- ➢ Select "All folders access" from the menu. You can view the applications that have access.
- ➢ To allow your phone to record the screenshot, enable the "Samsung capture" option from it.

If either the palm gesture technique or the virtual assistant Bixby are both disabled, your phone might not be capturing the screenshot. To assist you in taking a snapshot using either of those two techniques, enable both of them via settings.

Using the screen recorder on the Samsung smartphone

It is simple to record your computer's screen using the screen recorder, a novel feature that eliminates the need to download any extra software. You can initiate screen recording by clicking the icon in your Quick panel.

Using Screen Recordings

By scrolling down, choose Screen Recorder from your Quick Menu.

> ➢ After selecting your chosen Sound settings, click Start recording.

> ➢ After selecting your chosen Sound settings, click Start recording.

➤ For your Screen Recording, select from a variety of choices at the top of the screen.

➤ Simply tap the Stop icon button when you're ready to stop the movie.

➤ Allows you to decorate your video by writing or drawing on the screen with up to 8 different colors.

➤ Will activate or disable the Picture-in-Picture (PiP) feature, which allows you to record your own video as it plays over the screen.

➢ Tap the Stop button once the video has completed recording.
➢ Setting up the screen recorder differently

Making use of your Quick Options

1.To reach your Quick Settings, swipe down the screen and select "Screen Recorder"

2 After choosing your desired Sound and Video quality, click Done.

Making use of your Advanced Options

1 Enter your settings and select "Advanced Capabilities."

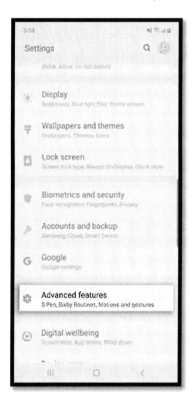

2 Pick the screen capture and screenshot options.

3 Select Screen Recorder Preferences.

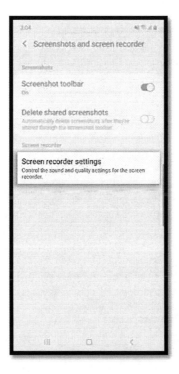

4 Choose the Selfie video size, Sound, and Video quality choices.

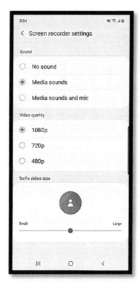

Please be aware that the selfie video size is supported in 5 levels (the selfie video is only for the front camera).

1. Find the My Files app's screen recordings

2. Select on Videos

3 Selected Screen Recordings

4.All stored screen recordings will then be viewable on your Galaxy Phone or Tablet.

Put screen recordings on a Flash card.

2.Click on Videos

Search for and choose the Screen Recordings subdirectory.

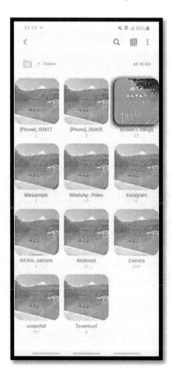

The screen recording movie can be chosen by long pressing it.

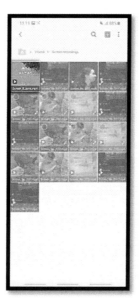

Select either Move or Duplicate.

To return to the main screen for My Files, click the arrow icon.

Hit on SD Card

Choose the location where you want to store the screen recording.

Select Copy here or Move here once you are satisfied with the file location of your screen recording.

Your screen recording video will be available for viewing on your SD Card once the transfer is finished.

CHAPTER EIGHTEEN

CALENDAR USAGE

Systematic planning and organizing can support your success when you manage your time well. Utilize the intuitive and useful Samsung Calendar app to learn how to manage your calendar. It has a number of features to organize your diary in order to meet your requirements and follow your routine.

Basic Calendar application navigation

It will be simpler for you to learn how to use the symbols if you are familiar with their definitions prior to using Calendar.

1. Menu: Click this link for more choices.

2. Date Select: Tap this to rapidly switch the day of the week, the month, and the year to jump to a particular date.

3. Drawing mode: On specific S-pen-equipped devices, this choice is only accessible when viewing the monthly view. Use drawing mode to annotate your schedule as if it were a wall-mounted calendar.

4. Today: Pressing this option will bring you right up to the present time.

  5. Events: The names of your activities are visible on the calendar itself.

To enlarge an event, tap on it.

6. **Selection box:** The date you've chosen date is indicated by the dashed lines drawn a date field. The calendar will instantly choose the current date

 when you open it.

7. Current date: To help you see it more easily, the current date will be emphasized.

8. Create an event by tapping this icon. The day that is presently chosen in the selection box will be used as the date of the event.

By swiping left or right, you can change the month that is presently displayed.

Slide up: To see more details about the date you've chosen, swipe up once or twice.

Steps for setting up the calendar

You can link to your calendar when you first launch the app using one of four accounts: your Samsung account, Exchange (Outlook), Google, or Microsoft account. After entering your email address and password, your previously made schedules will be synchronized.

How to change your calendar settings

1: Open the Calendar application, then choose Settings (three horizontal lines).

2.Click the Settings option

First day of the week: You can choose any one of the seven days to be the first day of the week.

Five different alternate schedules are available in Samsung Calendar. These are the Hijri, Shamsi, Vietnamese lunar, Chinese lunar, and Korean lunar months.

Show week numbers: Using this option, you can add a number to your calendar that indicates how many weeks there are.

Events that you refused to attend can be hidden.

Short occurrences can be highlighted: Events that happen quickly can be highlighted.

How to create an event

Step 3: Set the Start and Finish dates and times if you want to keep track of how long the event lasted.

Step 4: If required, enter the location and the alert types and settings (methods/timing/multiple alarm/repetition) before saving the event.

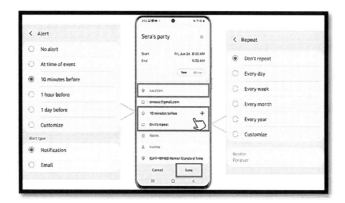

How to modify or remove an event

Step 1: Tap the date of the occasion you wish to modify or delete. Tap the date and hold it.

Step 2: Tap Delete or Edit to make detailed changes to the program.

Step 1: Launch the Calendar app, then select the day to which you want to add the plan.

Step 2: Tap the + icon to modify the event's title.

How to sync your calendar with recently added external accounts

Step 1: Open the Calendar application, then choose Settings (three horizontal lines).

Step 2: Select a letter and then tap the accounts.

Step 3: Select "Join now."

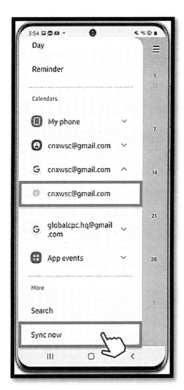

Calendar Sharing

Step 1: Select the person or group you want to share the information with. Tap the date and hold it.

Step 2: Select Share > Publish as Calendar File or Text from the menu.

CHAPTER NINETEEN

CALL MAKING WITH GOOGLE DUO

Before Beginning

- ❖ A voice or video discussion can be started.
- ❖ Make sure the Duo software is updated to the latest edition.
- ❖ Start the Google Duo app.
- ❖ Look up acquaintances or give the number at the top a call.
- ❖ Tap it to call a contact or number.

Make a decision:

- ❖ To begin a video chat, tap Call.
- ❖ To start an audio-only discussion, tap Voice call.
- ❖ Use Google Duo on a Google Home device.
- ❖ On your Android smartphone, open the Duo program.
- ❖ At the very top of your contact list, tap Contact Home.
- ❖ You can use Google Duo to make calls to any Google Home device that you have access to, including Smart Displays with Google Assistant.
- ❖ The group online conference can start now.
- ❖ Every member of the squad has their name displayed.

Group video conversations on Google Duo can have up to 32 participants.

Create A Group

- Start the Google Duo application.
- After New call, tap Create group in the bottom right area.
- Choose based on your relationships.
- Then click Done.
- Your video is presently on, if you want to mention it.
- Tap Video to turn on or off your recording.
- To start a video conversation, tap.
- The group could be given a moniker.
- Choose Change, enter a name, then choose Save.

Share a link to launch a conference session.

- ➢ Launch the Duo program.

- ➤ Tap Create group after new call in the lower right corner.
- ➤ Identify your connections.
- ➤ Click Done.
- ➤ Click or tap to add contacts or share
- ➤ Tap Copy or Share to share the URL with others or to add contacts.
- ➤ The recipient's computer will launch duo.google.com when they select the link.
- ➤ The Google Duo app starts if the recipient taps the link on a mobile device and has Google Duo installed.
- ➤ The link opens Google Duo in Google Play or the App Store if the recipient taps it on a mobile device and Google Duo isn't already loaded.
- ➤ Press Launch.

Call a current group or participate in a live group conversation.

Children's accounts cannot join groups unless at least one of their friends is a member of the group.

- ➤ Launch the Google Duo application.
- ➤ Tap New call in the lower right corner.
- ➤ Call a group or sign up for a live group under "Groups." The call is live and you can participate if the word "Live" appears next to the group name.
- ➤ To start a video call with an established group, tap the group name or any of the participants.
- ➤ Tap the group name or participants, then select Join video call to attend a live group call.
- ➤ Add people to a group, rename it, change the group link, or quit a group.
- ➤ Launch the Google Duo application.
- ➤ Tap New Call in the lower right corner.
- ➤ Tap a category under "Groups" and then "More options" More.
- ➤ Pick a choice, then adhere to the on-screen directions.

Suspect Groups

Google Duo flags a group as suspicious if it contains blocked users or individuals who are not in your contacts but are invited to a group. You won't receive any information from Google Duo regarding banned group members.

You can accept the organization or reject it. Google Duo won't unblock individuals you've blocked if you join.

Get rid of a group member
- Launch the Google Duo application.
- Tap New Call in the lower right corner.
- Tap a club under "Groups."
- To remove a contact, touch and retain it.

Tap to remove from group.

Additionally, you have the option to block the group user.

A word of caution: If the person you blocked tries to re-join the group by clicking the initial link, they are advised that the group does not exist. Access to the group link is refreshed for everyone else in the group.

Utilize Google Duo to make contacts from other applications

If video calling through your carrier is supported by both you and the person you are contacting

utilizing the same transport Your carrier's video service may be used during the conversation.

Have various carriers: Call is made with Google Duplex.

Whenever you want, you can use Wi-Fi or cellular data to talk to your loved ones in person. You can easily initiate video calls on your Samsung Galaxy phone using the Google Duo app. You don't even need to acquire the app for the majority of Android OS versions. Learn here how to initiate a video call using your Galaxy phone.

Note: Depending on the network provider and device type, Google Duo service availability may change.

Step 1: Launch the Phone program, then select the Keypad tab.

Step 2: After dialing the person's phone number to initiate a video call, press the Duo icon to the left of the phone icon.

As an alternative, you can call saved contacts via video straight from the Contact app. After choosing the person with whom you want to speak, press the Duo icon.

Note: The Google Duo icon may be replaced on some platforms by the video call icon.

A Wi-Fi network or cellular data connection must be used for both your phone and the phone being used to receive the info.

What if the standard video calling tool is not the Duo app?

Depending on your device model and whether the Duo app is the primary video calling app on your Galaxy phone:

On the Apps screen, look for the program in the Google folder. On the majority of Galaxy phones, the Duo app is already loaded.

If the program isn't already downloaded, do so from the Google Play Store.

Installing the Duo application

The Duo app needs extra setup at first, but it's simple. Just sign into your Google account and take a couple of quick steps.

Step 1: Choose your country and type in your phone number.

Step 2: Enter the Verification number after receiving it.

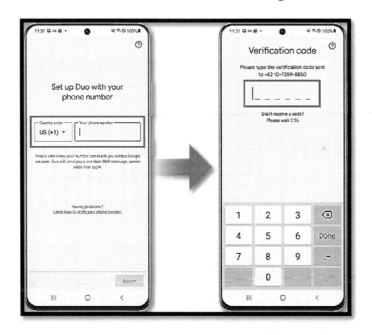

Note: Depending on the device model and program version, screenshots and menus may change.

GROUP VIDEO CALLS USING GOOGLE DUO

Search for Google Duo in the "Play Store" of your Samsung Galaxy S23 Ultra, select "Install," then click "Open" when the installation is finished. For use on your Android 13 device with One UI 5.1, you must have a Google account. If your Google account is already set up, you must log in without any issues. If you don't already have an account, you can establish one in a few minutes.

Simply launch Duo on your Galaxy S23 Ultra, and when it asks for permission to access your contacts on Samsung devices as well as the camera and microphone, select "allow" to start video calling. Your Samsung Galaxy S23 Ultra has GPS, GLONASS, BDS, and GALILEO, so it could ask for access to your position. You can choose to "Deny" if you don't want to give it access in order to make a video call. You will be prompted to input your phone number, which is required in order to communicate with other users and conduct video calls. You will then receive an SMS containing a confirmation code, which you must enter in Google Duo in order to proceed.

To make a call, you must look for a contact by name or phone number; if you can't find them, it's likely that they don't have the Google Duo app installed on their device. If this is the case, you can send them an invitation by clicking the "Invite friends" option.

To initiate a group video call, select "start" after creating the group by clicking "Create group". The group will then appear on the home screen.

It is not possible to join a video call after it has begun; you must first establish the group.

Making video calls from virtually any device that has a camera, microphone, and internet link is one of the benefits of Duo. Since the Galaxy S23 Ultra has an app for iOS and Android as well as a website that can be accessed from a laptop, desktop computer, or a smart display like the Google Nest, it has a Wi-Fi 802.11 a/b/g/n/ac/6e, tri-band, Wi-Fi Direct connection.

CHAPTER TWENTY

NOTES AND FILES APPS

Everybody relies on their phones and private notes. You can combine the best aspects of both realms with the Samsung Notes app on your phone. It enables you to take notes whenever you want on your phone and has some essential features and choices that you need to be aware of.

Functions and options for Samsung Notes

Samsung Notes may become disorganized if you've made a lot of notes on your phone. It has tools that will make organizing your notes much simpler, so don't worry.

For easier navigation, you could group your notes into various groups. Alternately, you can use a search engine to find notes with particular names or topics rather than going through all of your notes.

Some of Samsung Notes' most useful functions are listed below:

A variety of notes are displayed in Samsung Notes.

You can quickly highlight a portion of text before selecting an action. To highlight more text, hold down a sentence with your S Pen while dragging it.

The actions mentioned below are:

- The accessible options include Clone, Paste, Dictionary, Show Clipboard, and Share.
- Remember that this feature is only supported by the Note series.
- The screen can be zoomed in or out by simply touching it.
- Each device will have a distinct zoom limit.
- The search function to look up and find the specific note you need, use this feature. After clicking the Search button, enter your search keywords.

Put your notes in order:

- Several apps can be used to organize your notes.
- The passcode can be changed by going to Samsung Notes' settings, selecting Note unlock methods, and then selecting Change password.
- Locking notes requires a Samsung account.

Organize your notes:

You have so many papers that you can't tell which one is which. You can arrange them to make it easier for you to decide. Select your preferred choice, such as Date created, by tapping the Filter icon on the Samsung Notes home screen. Additionally, you can modify the general design of your notes. To alter the way the notes are displayed, touch More options (the three vertical dots), then tap View.

This tool makes action icons out of your handwritten notes. Simply tap the various icons to dial numbers, write emails, solve math problems, and access websites. Toggle the switch next to the Action icons after selecting Settings from the menu (the three horizontal lines in the upper left corner).

- ➢ After clicking More options, choose Edit (the three vertical dots).
- ➢ Choose the option you want, followed by the comments you want.
- ➢ To send them somewhere else, press Share.
- ➢ To move them to another folder, select Move.
- ➢ To remove them entirely from your phone, hit Delete.

Lock your notes: If you want to keep some notes secret, you can secure them (for example, your collection of poetry). Open the desired note, select More options (three vertical dots), and then select Lock. Then, after you have followed the on-screen directions, create a password for your memo.

Select the switch at the top of the screen to turn the feature on or off. Press Sync Notes data to decide whether synchronizing takes place over Wi-Fi, Wi-Fi, or mobile data.

If you want to save your note as a different kind of file, you have a lot of choices. It can be archived as a written document, image, PowerPoint presentation, PDF, Microsoft Word document, or PowerPoint presentation. Tap More options after choosing the memo you want to backup (the three vertical dots). After that, select the desired file type by tapping Save as file.

By syncing Samsung Notes with Microsoft OneNote, your notes are now synchronized with your Samsung account and accessible in Microsoft Office!

Importing and exporting data in Samsung Notes

Maybe your Google Drive notes aren't showing up in Samsung Notes. There's no need to fret because you can easily import them to your phone so they show up in the application.

Open the program, select Menu (the three horizontal lines), and then select the Settings icon to import data into Samsung Notes. To import notes, tap. To upload data, select the source (such as your Samsung account) and then follow the on-screen instructions.

Samsung Notes also allows you to load and export PDF files! The PDFs cannot be edited, but you can annotate or sketch on them using the app.

Update Samsung Notes

Keep Samsung Notes updated at all times in case any new note-taking features are introduced.

To access settings, open the program and select Menu (the three horizontal lines). Tap Update if one is accessible after selecting About Samsung Notes.

Samsung Notes can receive automatic updates from the Galaxy Store and Google Play Store so that they are always up to current.

Organize folders, templates, and note types.

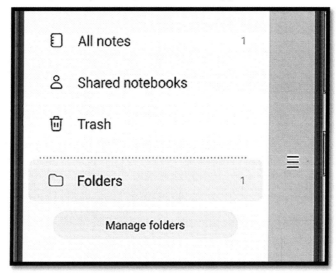

To ensure that you can always find what you need, maintain your Samsung Notes well-organized. The software offers a variety of options for structuring and formatting your notes.

To maintain consistency, group all of your connected notes in one folder or use the same template for all of them.

Share your notes

Did you use Samsung Notes to doodle a cute image or record crucial meeting information? Right from the app, you can email it as various file types to yourself, a friend, or a colleague. You could send the job notes as a Word or PDF document, for instance!

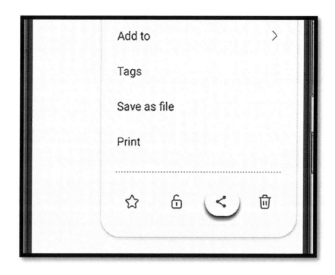

Select your preferred note in the Samsung Notes app, then tap More options (the three vertical dots).

Select the file format you want to use by tapping the Share icon. Samsung Notes files, PDF files, Microsoft Word files, Microsoft PowerPoint files, image files, and text files are all options.

Choose your preferred sharing method, such as text message, email, etc., after choosing the file format. Send the item next in the usual manner.

The Samsung Notes app has emphasized the Share icon.

Note: Some sharing choices do not allow the sending of certain files. Verify that the sharing method you chose is suitable for the file type.

Use handwriting functions

Samsung Notes supports writing with a S Pen. Simply pull out your S Pen and start writing a note in the program on a compatible phone. You can edit and transform your handwriting to text. You can still take notes using the keyboard or even your finger if the S Pen isn't your style.

S PEN APPLICATION
Learn the S pen's basics.

The S Pen is located on the left-bottom corner of the gadget. Push the S Pen until it clicks into place, then pull it out to use. You will be required to watch a short tutorial when using the S Pen for the first time before you can select Done.

Memos Written by Hand

1. To make the Air Command icon appear, tap a blank area of the screen with the S Pen or hover it over the screen. Select the Air Command symbol with the S Pen.

Note: By default, the air order icon will show up on the right side of the screen. Select the icon for Air Command and drag it to the desired position.

2. From the Air command screen, select create note. Create a note.

It should be noted that you can write a memo by hand without waking the gadget. Holding the S Pen close to the Always On Display panel, press the S Pen button. Fill out the page however you please, then select Save When Done. Any notes entered without waking the device will be instantly updated in Samsung Notes.

3. Type the email's body. When finished, select Save as file from the drop-down menu by clicking the menu icon, then pick the desired file type and storage location. Once completed, type the name of the memo you want, then click Save.

Note: Your memo will be immediately saved to Samsung Notes in addition to the save location you have chosen. Swipe up from the screen's center to reveal the Apps tray on the home screen to reach Samsung Notes. Select the

Samsung Notes program after navigating to it. On the home page, there will also be an icon for recent notes. Select the Note icon Samsung Note icon to see the most current note. Selecting and dragging the Note symbol Samsung Note icon to Remove at the bottom of the screen will remove a note from the home screen.

ON IMAGES, ADD TEXT OR DRAWINGS.

Choose screen write from the Air command interface. You can add text or images to a snapshot after it has been taken. Once you're done, click the Save button.

Utilize Smart Select.

You can screenshot particular areas of the screen using Quick Select. Choose the Smart Select icon from the Air command screen, then choose the desired shape for the outline and drag it across the screen to choose the desired picture capture. To save, click the Save button.

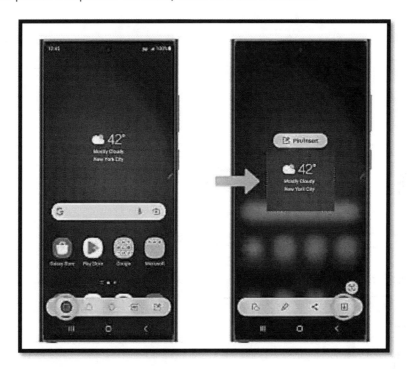

Open the S Pen's settings

Select the settings icon on the Air command page. Change the parameters as needed.

Note: You can also swipe down from the notification area, select Settings from the menu, scroll to Advanced Features, and then choose S Pen.

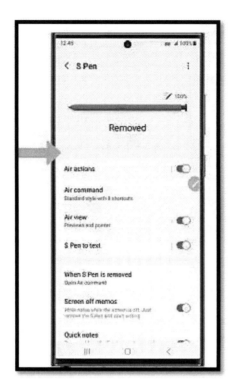

Shortcuts for editing Air commands

1. Choose Air command, then Shortcuts, from the S Pen interface.

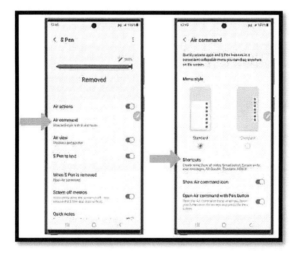

2. To add an app to the Air command interface, select it and drag it there. On the Air command screen, click the Remove icon next to the program you want to delete.

Set Air view to on or off.

By moving your pen over the screen, you can use Air View to examine data, expand text, or enlarge images. The Air view switch is found on the S Pen settings page.

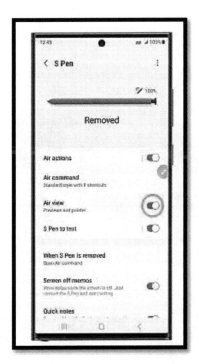

Merge the S Pen

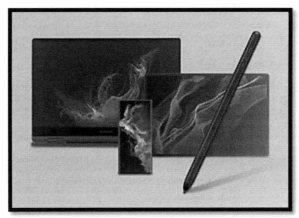

The S Pen has a 30-foot working range. When you leave this area, the S Pen will stop communicating with your phone.

A unique and advanced Bluetooth that transmits a signal at a very low frequency is built into the S Pen. As a result, it doesn't require pairing with your phone like other Bluetooth gadgets do. You won't need to continually pair and unpair the S Pen and phone because the Bluetooth connection is strong enough to maintain it.

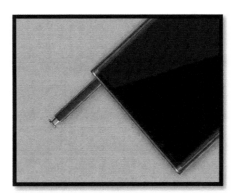

Simply place the S Pen into your phone for a few seconds to restore connectivity if it becomes gone. It pairs quickly, and the connection is soon restored. You must hit the Pairing button if you are using a S Pen Pro.

Check out our troubleshooting instructions if you encounter any connection issues when using your S Pen.

Charge the S Pen

The S Pen is made to last, but if you leave it outside of your phone for more than 30 minutes or if you press the Pen button frequently, its battery can run out (about 200 times). Your S Pen will power for 40 seconds inside your phone after you insert it. In that time, it will fully refresh. Or, if you have a S Pen Pro, you can charge it with a USB-C cable.

How will you know if the phone needs to be charged, though? Don't fear, a notification will be sent to you when your S Pen's battery level reaches about 20% to remind you to charge it.

S PEN REMOTE PREFERENCES OPTIONS

You can reach the Air command menu and check the S Pen's battery level at any time by removing the S Pen from your device. Click Settings in the lower left corner after that. Your S Pen's remaining battery life will be displayed at the top of the screen. If you're experiencing trouble getting your S Pen to charge, we can help. Start over or look for the S Stylus

Resetting your S Pen will restore all of its functions, including remote controls, to their default settings.

You can try looking for your S Pen or resetting it if it won't link to your phone or doesn't appear to be charging.

Navigate to Preferences, click on it, then look for and choose S Pen.

Tap S Pen once more, then select More choices (the three vertical dots).

Your phone will start searching for the S Pen when you tap Scan for S Pen Pro. If necessary, adhere to the directions displayed on screen.

Tap Reset S Pen and wait for the S Pen to restart itself if that doesn't help. Keep in mind that resetting the S Pen will restore it to its factory defaults.

Use the S Pen Fold Edition

You can use the S Pen Fold Version with a Z Fold3 or the newest Z Fold4! When you remove it from the case and begin using it, it will instantly connect with your phone. Like other S Pens, this one does not require charging, so you can use it for extended periods of time to take notes or explore your screen.

CAPTURING A VIDEO TO GENERATE GIFs

On your Galaxy phone, you can rapidly create GIF images from the photos that are stored in your photo album. Directly from the camera app or from the pictures you captured, you can make a GIF image. For a summary of various ways to make GIFs, see below.

Create a GIF image from a collection of images.

You can create amusing GIF images using your own photos by using the Gallery program. Unlike videos, GIFs are picture formats that have been heavily compressed and mimic short animations. The first step in making a GIF is combining the pictures that have been saved in the Gallery app.

To combine several images into one GIF, simply follow the steps listed below:

Step 1: Launch the Gallery app and long-press numerous photos to select them all.

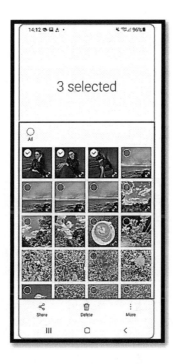

You can watch the generated GIF in your Gallery app after saving.

The burst mode, also known as continuous shooting mode, is a function of the camera on your Galaxy phone that allows you to quickly take multiple pictures by swiping down on the shutter button. It might appear like a smoother animation if you create a GIF picture from the burst shots that were taken.

To convert a burst photo into a GIF, follow the steps listed below:

Step 1: Launch the Gallery app, then select the burst shot you want to convert to a GIF from.

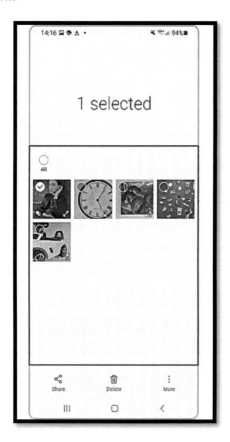

How to snap a burst of shots

Step 1: Launch the Camera app and confirm that PHOTO is chosen as your camera mode.

Step 2: To stop a burst of shots, swipe down on the shutter button and then let go of it.

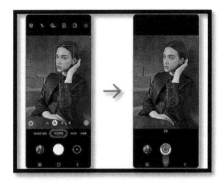

Note: You may need to adjust the Swipe Shutter Button settings if you notice that a GIF rather than a burst photo is being taken. Enter your camera's settings, press the Swipe Shutter button, and then choose Take Burst shot.

Make a GIF right away by using the Camera app

By using simple camera settings, you can create GIF images straight from the Camera app. The Gallery app lets you view GIF images that you've taken with your camera.

To modify the camera settings, adhere to the methods below:

Step 1: Launch the Camera application and then press the Settings button in the top left corner.

Note: Based on the device model and program version, the menu and screenshots may differ.

CHAPTER TWENTY-ONE

HEALTH APP FOR SAMSUNG

If you want to monitor your health or merely stay as fit as you can, the Samsung Health Monitor app is for you. Together with your Galaxy watch and phone, you can use it to record and share your ECG rhythm with your healthcare practitioner. You must first launch the app and then synchronize your devices using Bluetooth and the Galaxy Wearable app before you can begin capturing your ECG.

The ECG app should not be used by anyone under the age of 22, and people with known arrhythmias other than atrial fibrillation should not use it in place of more established methods of diagnosis or therapy. Users should contact a licensed healthcare professional before interpreting or acting clinically based on the device output.

Pair watch and phone together

To use the ECG function in the Samsung Health Monitor app, you must first pair your watch and phone if you haven't already. Your devices can be linked using the Galaxy Wearable software.

After accessing Quick settings by swiping down from the top of your phone's screen, hit the Bluetooth icon to enable Bluetooth.

Next, travel there by opening the Galaxy Wearable app on your phone. Select Launch after that.

Pick your preferred watch style from the available choices. Either wait for the connection from your watch, or select Scan again to search for it.

Follow the on-screen instructions to finish connecting your watch and phone.

Download and install the Samsung Health Check program.

Once your phone and watch have been paired, you can start setting up the ECG feature of your watch using the Samsung Health Monitor app. The Samsung Health Monitor App cannot be purchased individually. It can only be used after updating all of your applications and pairing your Galaxy phone with a watch that is compatible. There are some extra steps that can be taken if the app is still not displaying.

Note: To use the Samsung Health Monitor app, you must have either a Galaxy Watch Active2 or Watch3 running the most current software (Tizen 4.0.0.8 or higher) or a Galaxy Watch4 connected to a Galaxy phone running Android 7 (Nougat) or later.

Open the Samsung Health Monitor tab by navigating to it on your connected phone.

After selecting Install, let the application download.

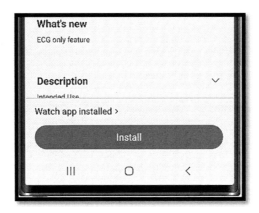

> ➤ When it's done, tap Open, then read the information that is given. Hit "accept."
> ➤ You will then be prompted to grant a few rights. At the top of the screen, select All rights by tapping the switch, and then select Done.
> ➤ Tap Continue after filling out the form to establish your profile. The software will start looking for a smart watch that works with it.
> ➤ Tap Get began when the phone recognizes your watch. Open the Samsung Health Monitor app on your watch if your phone is having difficulty locating your watch. Click Accept Permissions, then select Launch Phone App. The watch should then be found by your phone.
> ➤ The basic setup of the app will be required of you. Review the displayed material and adhere to the on-screen instructions. When you're done, tap Done.

Read the details on the watch, then tap OK. After that, your watch will prompt you to take an ECG measurement. You have the option of doing it right away or afterward.

The Galaxy Wearable application has been updated.

For your watch to sync correctly, make sure the Galaxy Wearable software on your phone has been updated.

The most recent software is also required to use the ECG feature, and the Samsung Health Monitor App cannot be downloaded separately. It can only be used after updating all of your applications and pairing your Galaxy phone with a watch that is compatible. You can update the Galaxy Wearable software from the Galaxy Store or Play Store.

Note: A Galaxy Watch Active2 or Watch3 running the most current software (Tizen 4.0.0.8 or higher), or a Galaxy Watch4 paired with an Android 7 (Nougat) or later Galaxy phone, are required to use the Samsung Health Monitor app.

Open the Galaxy Store on your phone by navigating there and tapping it. Then press Menu (the three horizontal lines).

To view all of your apps, select My apps or Updates to see any updates that are currently accessible.

Next, select the Galaxy Wearable Update icon.

CHAPTER TWENTY-TWO

SAMSUNG PAY

Since you're probably holding your phone in your palm while shopping, use it to make in-store transactions. With Samsung Pay, you can immediately add credit cards to your phone and use them to make purchases in stores or even restaurants. You can easily return items you've purchased using your digital card number.

Use the application to pay using it

Using Samsung Pay, you can make transactions without digging through your wallet.

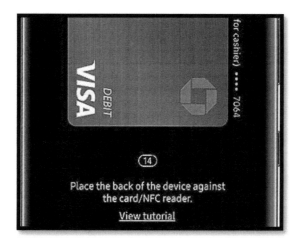

When you're ready to make a transaction, open Samsung Pay on your phone. Tap the Pay icon to select your preferred card. Once more, tap Pay, and then choose the degree of security you desire, such as providing a PIN or using your fingerprints. Put your finger on the fingerprint scanner on your phone or enter the required security information. Hold the back of your phone in front of the contactless scanner to complete your purchase, then complete the required steps.

Guidelines for Back of the gadget should be against card reader or NFC reader. If your phone's Favorite Cards function is activated, you can access your cards even faster.

Note: If a transaction fails to complete, you can get help from our transaction guide.

Use the cards you prefer to pay.

- ➢ Swipe up from the bottom of the screen to pay with one of your Preferred Cards.
- ➢ Next, swipe the cards to choose your favored one.
- ➢ Choose the card you desire.
- ➢ Select your preferred protection method, such as entering your PIN or using your fingerprints, after tapping Pay.
- ➢ Enter the necessary security information, or just put your finger on the fingerprint scanner on your phone.
- ➢ To finish your buy, hold the back of your phone in front of the contactless reader and take the necessary actions.

Make a transaction using a Galaxy watch

On your Galaxy watch, you can also quickly make in-store transactions using Samsung Pay. Before you start making in-store purchases, just make sure your watch is set up for Samsung Pay.

To open Samsung, Pay on your watch, click and hold the Back button.

Next, locate the chosen card by either rotating the bezel or swiping on the screen.

Hold the wrist with the watch on it close to an NFC scanner or a payment terminal. If you're experiencing issues, make sure the watch is positioned at least an inch away from the terminal.

Make a payment using a gift card

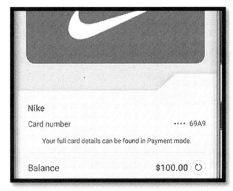

Gift cards can also be used in Samsung Pay to make in-store transactions.

However, if the clerk requests it at checkout, you might need to show them your gift card's number or barcode.

Return your purchase

If you want to return the object, go back to the shop where you bought it.

But before going to the cashier, make sure you have the ticket. The cashier needs to know where to find the digital card details so they can use it. Even if you have the number, it's possible that some shops will still require you to open Samsung Pay and place your phone near to the NFC reader in order to complete the refund.

A purchase that cannot be reversed

The digital card number may have changed if you are trying to return something you purchased using Samsung Pay but it is not being accepted. If you changed devices since making your transaction or if you deregistered and then reregistered your card afterward, the number will change.

Out of worry for security, no copy of the authentic digital card information is stored in Samsung Pay or on any Samsung Pay servers. You won't be able to get the card number you had before it was changed as a consequence.

When you make a return using a new digital card number, request that the retailer process it the same way they would if your physical card were changed. If you have any issues filing your return or require additional assistance, get in touch with your card's provider.

How should I arrange the menu icons in my Samsung Wallet Quick Access?

You can choose to swiftly and simply manage your favorite cards with Samsung Wallet. With the help of its quick access tab feature, you won't need to bring physical cards around with you since you can access your cards from the lock or home screens as well as when your screen is off.

You can easily access your favorite cards, add or remove them, or reorder them using Samsung Wallet. Just take the following actions to do it:

Delete or add cards to the Quick Access group

Your entire collection of enrolled credit and debit cards are instantly added to the Quick Access tab. However, you can always add or remove your favorite cards.

Follow these procedures to accomplish this:

1.Swipe one of the Quick Access menu cards down in Samsung Wallet once it is open.

2 In the lower right corner of the screen, select the Edit Quick Access menu.

3 Tap the cards under the Quick Access option.

4.The cards you want to use as Fast Access tab cards can be selected or deselected.

Note that a maximum of 40 cards can be put up as Quick Access tab cards.

Quick access and default card

Swipe up from the bottom of the screen to bring up the Quick Access tab cards for rapid access to your payment cards. From the Home screen, the Lock screen, or when your screen is off, you can view them.

Follow these methods to alter where the various Quick Access tab cards are displayed:

1.Start your Samsung Wallet app, then select the icon with three lines (menu).

2 Tap the settings symbol (cogwheel), then choose "Quick Access and preset card."

3 To enable or disable quick access for that screen, tap the switch next to the places you want to use.

Order the Quick Access tab elements differently

You can reorder the Quick Access tab tiles to make things even simpler.

Just take the following actions to do it:

1.Swipe one of the Quick Access menu cards down after opening Samsung Pay Wallet.

2.Touch a card, hold it in place, and then move it to the desired spot. The positions of the cards will change instantly.

Regardless of the order of the cards, the last card you used will immediately be displayed when you access this tab.

With Samsung Pay, you can buy and use gift cards.

All people adore gift cards. And thanks to Samsung Pay, you can purchase gift cards from various retailers and use them directly in the app, eliminating the need to carry around a whole deck of them. Gift vouchers can also be added indefinitely to your Samsung Pay account. Or, add funds to a physical gift card you have already purchased.

Make a gift card purchase for yourself

Buy a gift certificate with Samsung Pay and use it however you like if you want to treat yourself.

➢ Open Samsung Pay, tap the three horizontal lines to access the menu, and then choose Gift card store.
➢ Use the search box to find the gift card you're looking for. Alternatively, you can scroll up and down to view the gift cards that are offered.

Choose the gift card of your choice and the monetary value you want.

Select For me, then select Add to Wallet. On the following screen, click Check Out.

At the top, make sure Samsung Pay is chosen, and then tap Pay with SAMSUNG Pay.

Additionally, you might need to select PIN or IRIS before entering the necessary security information. Simply put your finger on the fingerprint scanner on your phone if you have fingerprint security enabled.

Your gift card will be accessible in Samsung Pay after your purchase has been verified. You'll receive an email with it as well. The gift card is now usable for transactions.

Buy a friend a gift card.

Never again struggle with the dilemma of what to give someone.

➢ You can buy digital gift cards through Samsung Pay and present them to friends.

➢ Open Samsung Pay, press the three horizontal lines to access the menu, and then choose Gift card store.

➢ Use the search box to find the gift card you're looking for. Alternatively, you can scroll up and down to view the gift cards that are offered.

Choose the gift certificate of your choice and the monetary value you want. Next, select For a Friend and fill in their details. Click "Add to Basket."

Click Check Out on the subsequent screen to proceed. Make sure Samsung Pay is selected at the top, then press Pay with SAMSUNG Pay.

Prior to entering the required security details, you might also need to choose PIN or IRIS. If your phone has fingerprint security activated, all you have to do is place your finger on the scanner.

If your acquaintance uses Samsung Pay, they will receive the gift credit in their Samsung Pay app. It will also be sent to them via email.

If you purchased a gift card for someone who does not use Samsung Pay, they will get it via email. They can use their gift card to make a purchase by clicking the provided link and printing a duplicate of the gift card.

Use a gift card to make a purchase

Perhaps you recently celebrated your birthday and got a gift certificate in the mail. You can buy something with it after you add it to your pocket!

Internet payment

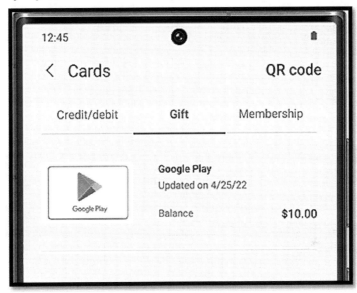

Open Samsung Pay by going there, then press Menu (the three horizontal lines).

After selecting Cards, select the Gift option at the top.

Choose the gift card of your choice from there. Enter the required security details after tapping Pay.

To complete the purchase, adhere to the on-screen directions.

CHAPTER TWENTY-THREE

SAMSUNG DEX

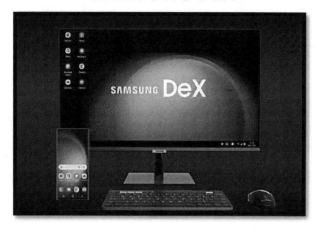

One of the most unexpected and useful features on Galaxy smartphones and tablets is Samsung DeX, which allows you to expand your mobile device to a larger screen and mimic a desktop environment. Once your device is connected to a display, you can use multiple apps at once and resize windows just like you would on a PC.

DeX initially required an HDMI adapter in order to connect your Galaxy phone or tablet with your display. The tough Tab Active 4, the Galaxy Z Fold 4 5G, and other more recent Samsung mobile devices, however, enable you to operate DeX wirelessly on any monitor that supports Miracast, creating an even more seamless working environment. On Samsung Smart TVs, this is useful for demonstrations and other tasks requiring a sizable canvas.

Additionally, Samsung has a selection of Smart Monitors that support Bluetooth DeX for a more traditional desktop environment. With the aid of a Bluetooth keypad and mouse, you can now create a straightforward DeX setup to finish your workday without ever turning on a PC or plugging in a cable. Of course, you can still use DeX if you don't have a Smart Monitor or a Miracast-capable monitor. Simply attach to a USB-C monitor directly or use an HDMI to USB-C adapter.

However, here's how to set up Bluetooth DeX on your Samsung Smart Monitor if you do want to use it:

The process of installing Samsung DeX on your Samsung Smart Display

➢ Plug in your Smart Monitor and switch it on to get started.
➢ Select the Source option and pick Screen Mirroring using the provided remote control or the physical buttons on the display.
➢ Drag the quick menu down from the top of your Galaxy device's screen, then select the DeX choice.
➢ "DeX on TV or Monitor" should be chosen from the DeX interface.
➢ To connect with displays, your Galaxy smartphone will look for them. Tap on your Smart Monitor when you see it show.
➢ I'm done now! The DeX logo will now show on your Smart Monitor, and you can start working right away.

You can use your mobile device as a touchpad if DeX is activated. However, you'll probably want to add a Bluetooth keypad and mouse for a truly desktop-like experience.

Adding a PC and mouse

➢ Use the keypad and mouse in pairing mode by following the manufacturer's instructions.
➢ Navigate to the Bluetooth option in your smartphone's Settings app.
➢ You can select the keypad and mouse from the Bluetooth options.
➢ You might need to type a verification number on your keypad in order to complete pairing.

Once they are connected, you can use your DeX-capable computer to work in your preferred productivity programs, such as Microsoft Office, Citrix Workspace, Microsoft Remote Desktop, Zoom Cloud Meetings, Cisco WebEx, Google Workspace, and others.

How to make calls and send messages using other Galaxy devices

Using the "Call & text on other devices" function, you can make and receive calls or send messages on your tablet. The same Samsung account that you use for your phone must be checked in with in order to activate Call & Text on Other Devices. Follow the guidelines below to activate and use this feature.

Set up the "Call and text on other smartphones" feature.

Using the Call & text on other devices feature, a Samsung account-based tool, calls and texts are forwarded and synced between your Samsung devices. You can use the number from your phone to make calls, send texts, and receive calls on your other Samsung devices. Your Galaxy tablet and phone both need to have the Call & Text on Other Devices feature activated, and both need to be signed into the same Samsung account.

Step 1: Open the Settings program, and then choose Advanced features.

Step 2: Toggle Call & text on other devices on by tapping the button next to it.

Or you can use the Quick panel to enable Call & SMS on other devices.

Automatic communication will take place. On your tablet, you can now place and receive calls as well as exchange messages.

Note: On some models from other carriers, the call and text feature might not be accessible.

Only when the phone is in the same nation or area as the tablet can it be used to call and text on other devices.

How to use your smartphone to make calls

If your tablet is closer to you than your phone and you receive a call, just welcome it there. Instead of using a phone, having a discussion on a tablet is very easy. When you see an incoming contact on your tablet, just swipe the green "Answer" icon to accept it. You can reject a call by pressing the red "Hang up" icon and calling the caller back or sending them a message by swiping up from the bottom of the screen.

Tap Pull call on the phone itself if you'd prefer to speak on it. By doing this, the call will stop on the tablet and start again on the phone.

CHAPTER TWENTY-TWO

DIFFERENT TIPS AND TRCKS ON SAMSUNG GALAXY S23 ULTRA

Display advice

There are two display modes available:

1.Adaptive

2.Standard.

open the 120Hz setting. While the normal setting sticks to 60Hz, adaptive smoothness will choose the appropriate refresh rate from 1-120Hz (on the Ultra, or 48-120Hz on the S23). Faster refresh can drain the charge more, but the images are smoother and move more quickly.

Adaptive technology has the advantage of taking care of your battery requirements. Configuration > Display > Animation Options exist for smoothness.

Three distinct display resolutions are available on the Galaxy S23 Ultra: WQHD+ (3088 x 1440), FHD+ (2316 x 1080), and HD+ (1544 x 720).

- Go to settings > display > screen resolution to access these choices.
- Select display from the settings page to enable dark mode.
- Under "Light" and "Dark" at the top of the website, you can find it.

302

- You can plan dark mode by clicking the "Dark mode settings" link underneath these visual examples.
- To alter the monitor's colors, go to settings > display > screen mode.
- Here, you can change the display's appearance from Vivid to Natural and directly alter the white balance between warm and cool.
- There are sophisticated settings that let you adjust the red, green, and blue channels individually if you want to go very deep.

Activate the video booster: A video enhancer that comes with the S23 Ultra aims to make viewing videos more enjoyable. It is compatible with a number of applications, such as Netflix, Amazon Video, and YouTube. Go to settings > advanced features to adjust the video brightness. Between Average and Bright are your options.

By changing the color of the display, the eye comfort shield should theoretically lessen blue light, shield against eye fatigue, and enhance slumber. By selecting preferences > display, "Eye Comfort Shield" can be activated. By clicking into this option and locating the adaptive or custom settings, you can decide whether to have it on all the time or just from a certain time.

One-handed mode: Choose "One-handed mode" under Settings > Advanced Features. This will make the display smaller so you can see items closer to the top more easily. This is ideal for people with little hands using large phones. Tap the arrows to move from left to right once in one-handed mode. Simply tap on the dark area to go out of one-handed mode.

Go to settings > display > edge panels to add or remove edge panels. You can add or remove the panels you don't want by tapping on Panels within this. You will then view the available option of panels. You'll spend more time navigating and less time actually doing if you stay with the useful.

You can change the edge panel handle to any location on the left or right of the screen. This is the handle that you must swipe to access the edge panels. You may move it around by simply pressing and holding. You can lock the location in the settings if you don't want to be able to move it, as seen below.

The edge panel handle's size and transparency can be altered: Go the settings menu and choose display > edge panels > handle. Under these options, you can alter the handle's appearance, including its color, size, and, if you choose, whether or not it vibrates when touched.

- Go to settings > display > edge panel to turn off the edge panels. Toggle it off to make the shortcut disappear.

The S23 Ultra with the S Pen: How to use the S Pen: There is a S Pen included with the S23 Ultra. Instead, than using a finger to interact with the display, just pop it out. There is a small transparent launcher to the center right of the screen that may be used to load its many compatible apps. This launcher provides access to Create note, View all notes, Smart choose, Screen write, Live messaging, AR Doodle, Translate, PENUP, and the possibility to add more interactions.

TIPS & TRICKS FOR NOTIFICATIONS

1.To disable an app's alerts, go to settings > notifications > app notifications. Here, you can examine the full list of available apps and activate notifications for each one.

2.Show badges for program icons: Each program on Android can show you how many notifications you have, which is one of its features. Samsung has applied this everywhere. Go to settings > notifications > advanced options and turn "App icon badges" off if you don't want it. Use this option to choose whether the notification displays as just a dot or a dot with numbers to show how many notifications there are.

3.You can examine your app notifications by holding down on an app shortcut for a long time: This extender for the icon badge is quite complex. When you touch and hold an app icon with a badge visible, a pop-up menu displaying the notifications will appear. By going to settings > notifications > app icon badges, you can toggle this choice at the foot of the page.

4.Using a tool that comes with Android, you can turn off a notification that you've gotten. If you want to change how a notification is delivered or, if you have already gotten one, to stop receiving more, press and hold it. You will be offered alternatives, such as "turn off notifications," when it expands.

5.By choosing "Settings," you'll enter a comprehensive menu where you may adjust any setting.

GAME-BOOSTING ADVICE

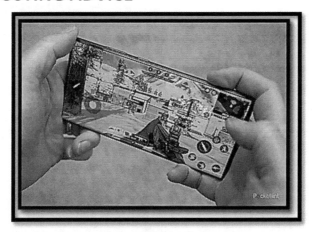

Reduce the update rate to save battery: To open the Game Launcher app, use the triple-line menu in the bottom right corner.

- From the menu that opens, select "Game Booster". When you choose "Low refresh rate," the refresh rate will then be set to 48Hz while you're playing games to preserve battery life.
- To avoid accidentally quitting a game while playing because your swipes were misinterpreted, blocking game navigation gestures is essential.
- Choosing "Block during game" after accessing the Game Booster options as previously mentioned.
- If you're using Android's softkeys, it will obviously be grayed out, but you can deactivate navigation gestures here.
- To exit a game, you need to tap twice.

- Turning off adaptive brightness will prevent your screen from fading while you play video games, which is the most annoying scenario.
- You can select to turn off auto brightness from the option displayed above to get around this problem.

Turn on Dolby Surround for gaming: In the options window, select Sound Quality and Effects under Noises and Vibrations. Here you can see the toggle for "Dolby Atmos for gameplay".

How to record a screen: A built-in screen recorder for the S23 Ultra model can be accessed through quick settings. Just swipe down, then scroll once more to see the extra 18 buttons. Select Screen camera from here.

To change the specifications, such as the video quality and sound (from the media and/or mic or none), press and hold this symbol.

PHOTO AND CAMERA TIPS

The S23 Ultra is the best of the three S23 devices in terms of camera quality.

Turn on the 200MP option (only for the S23 Ultra): The S23 Ultra's 200-megapixel camera is preconfigured to produce 12-megapixel images.

When pressing the aspect ratio button in the Camera app, choose "3:4 200MP" if you want the maximum resolution.

Turn on 8K video capture: Tap the quality icon to discover the 8K 30 option after opening the video mode in the Camera app. You'll be able to capture videos at their highest resolution thanks to this.

- To assess the scenario and propose the best composition, use the shot suggestions mode. The S10 was the first device to give this feature.
- The camera will suggest the best shot for you to capture using an on-screen guide.
- By launching the Camera program and tapping the settings cog, you can turn it on.

Utilize the scene enhancer to enhance your photos: Longer handheld nighttime pictures are possible with the scene optimizer, which uses artificial intelligence (AI) to improve your photos.

- Select the settings code in the upper left corner of the Camera app to turn **"Scene optimizer"** on.
- Use night setting to enhance your low-light photography.
- When a yellow crest moon symbol shows in the Camera app's viewfinder, night mode is active.
- When there is little light, the night mode automatically activates and records long exposures.
- When the outline of this moon symbol is made white, it can be touched to switch it off.

How to leave a mode: It's not instantly obvious how to return to default after selecting a camera mode, such as one from the "More" menu. If gesture control is activated, the only way to return to the standard viewfinder is to swipe back or touch the arrow next to the camera option.

- Rapid video initiation the side button must normally be double-pressed in order to activate the camera.
- To change this to, say, launch a different application, navigate to settings > advanced features > side key.

Swiping left or right in the Camera app's screen changes the camera's mode:

- You are not restricted to the default options shown above, which have Portrait to the left, Video and More to the right, and Picture as the default. You can add or remove camera modes that you find more useful.
- You can add more by clicking the "Add+" in the lower right corner of More. If you tap it, you can drag the desired modes onto the swipe-able bar so that you won't need to access More to make a selection.
- Use the up/down arrows in the Camera app to easily move between the front and back cameras. You can also change the cameras by pressing the power icon two more times.

By choosing the option to store DNG files in addition to regular JPEG files in the Camera app's settings > advanced photo choices > pro mode image format, you can enable RAW capture. You have the choice to save RAW settings when shooting in pro mode.

Shot in Expert RAW mode: To give you more control, Samsung features a unique Export RAW mode that is intended to be utilized with Lightroom. It provides 12MP RAW files, or 50MP RAW on the S23 Ultra. Swipe through the modes in the camera app to find more. You may need to download the app from the Galaxy Store to see Expert RAW as an option. Both the Samsung Gallery and Google Pictures apps will label photos that were taken in RAW.

Taking A Screenshot

There are numerous methods for taking screenshots on the Galaxy S23; you can use those recommended below or refer to this comprehensive tutorial.

Get a screenshot: Pressing the standby and volume down keys simultaneously shouldn't last too long or the power-off screen will appear.

To take a screenshot, use your palm to sweep the edge of the screen rather than using any buttons. Palm swipe to capture can be disabled under settings > advanced features > motions & gestures.

TIPS FOR TAKING PHOTOS

Whether you're a seasoned shooter or a beginner, you can use our guidance to capture beautiful images of your family.

1.If you want your photos to have a warm glow, think about shooting them during the golden hour, which is the time just after sunrise or before sunset. There are various golden hours that vary according to the time of year and your location.

2.If you're inside, try taking photos close to a window or another source of natural light.

3.Using three horizontal and three vertical lines to divide the picture into nine equal parts, the rule of thirds states that your subject or focal point should be in the left or right third of the frame. This is an excellent way to put together an eye-catching image! Your Galaxy phone can even create the rule of thirds matrix for you! Select the Camera app and press the Settings button to launch it. Next, tap the switch in the area with the Grid lines. Once you have seen the screen's horizontal and vertical lines, turn back to the camera.

4.If you don't want to get a fully candid shot, make sure your subject is relaxed and ready for the photograph. A relaxed stance and face expression are frequently easier to photograph.

NOTICE! NOTICE!! NOTICE!!!

WE WILL GREATLY APPRECIATE YOUR KIND REVIEW OF THIS BOOK

OTHER BOOKS WRITTEN BY GOLDEN MCPHERSON

1. PROCREATE 2023 FOR BEGINNERS AND PROS

2. IOS 16 USER GUIDE

3. QUICKBOOKS 2023 ALL-IN-ONE FOR BEGINNERS AND SENIORS

4. EVERYTHING WINDOWS 11 FOR SENIORS

5. ADOBE PREMIERE PRO 2023 FOR SENIORS

6. CAMERA GUIDE FOR SAMSUNG GALAXY S23 ULTRA

INDEX

Albums, 224, 225, 226, 231
battery life, 157
Biometrics, 178, 181, 182, 183, 184, 186, 199, 200, 202, 204
Bixby, 9, 10, 22, 239, 240
Bluetooth, 20, 90, 149, 150, 152, 153, 278, 299
Calendar, 256, 258
Cellular preferred,", 80
charging, 140, 147, 279, 280
Chrome browser, 206
Dark mode, 136, 137, 138
Dashboard, 186, 187
deactivate, 14, 20, 59, 138, 139, 154, 155, 171, 197, 211
Digital Wellbeing, 186, 189
Dolby Atmos, 145, 148
Download, 193, 233
Edge panels., 62
Equalizer, 148, 149
fingerprint, 177, 180, 181, 182, 183, 196, 289, 295
Flight mode, 20
folder, 44, 45, 46, 55, 72, 76, 78, 90, 110, 113, 116, 123, 125, 127, 129, 131, 134, 200, 201, 202, 206, 207, 263, 270
gadgets, 153, 278
Gallery, 43, 44, 201, 202, 218, 222, 224, 225, 226, 227, 228, 229, 230, 231, 234, 235, 281, 282, 308
Gmail, 158, 206, 207
Google, 90, 91, 100, 105, 110, 158, 159, 190, 192, 193, 194, 198, 206, 228, 260, 261, 262, 263, 264, 265, 270, 299, 308

Google Assistant, 159
Google Duo, 90, 91, 260, 261, 262, 264, 265
GPS antenna, 22
hotspots, 164
Hyperlapse, 220
Internet payment, 297
Link to Windows,, 207
Messages, 77, 88, 110, 113, 116, 123, 125, 127, 129, 131, 134, 206
Microsoft, 73, 206, 207, 231, 271, 299
MicroUSB, 70
Nightography, 216
notifications, 57, 59, 60, 87, 147, 149, 150, 170, 188
OneDrive, 207, 231, 232, 233, 235
Outlook, 73, 207
Panorama, 220
parental controls, 190
permissions, 31, 200, 230
Quick Settings, 9, 12, 13, 16, 18, 20, 153, 155, 165, 202, 243
RAW, 218, 221, 222, 308
Ringtones, 87
S Pen, 272, 275, 276, 277, 278, 279, 280
S23 Ultra, 22, 68, 73, 74, 77, 78, 139, 154, 236, 264, 265, 306, 308
Samsung Galaxy, 10, 73, 79, 151, 152, 261, 264
Samsung Pay, 290, 293, 294, 295, 296, 297
screenshot, 236, 237, 238, 239, 240, 245, 275, 308
SD Card, 251, 252

security, 158, 165, 169, 170, 177, 178, 181, 182, 183, 184, 185, 198, 199, 200, 202, 203, 204, 289, 295, 297

selfies, 199, 216, 231

sensor, 180, 181

shooting modes., 219

shortcuts, 46, 47, 50

Side key, 10, 22

smartphone, 105, 119, 136, 154, 159, 170, 182, 206, 299

transparency, 47

unlock, 70, 168, 169, 170, 181, 182, 186, 267

upscaler, 149

video calls, 31, 89, 91, 261, 265

voicemail, 93, 94, 95, 134

wallpaper, 30, 43, 44, 57

Widgets, 46, 47, 57

Wi-Fi, 20, 71, 79, 80, 156, 157, 159, 164, 206, 261, 262, 265

Manufactured by Amazon.ca
Bolton, ON